CREATIVE THINKING

In the Decision and Management Sciences

JAMES R. EVANS

University of Cincinnati

COLLEGE DIVISION South-Western Publishing Co.

CINCINNATI   DALLAS   LIVERMORE

To Joe Cieply, Tom Hill, Don Phillips, and John Jarvis,
whose creative influences have had lasting impact.

Sponsoring Editor: James M. Keefe
Production Editor: Sharon L. Smith
Production House: Impressions Publishing Services
Cover and Interior Designer: Craig LaGesse Ramsdell
Marketing Manager: Scott Person

MI60AA
Copyright © 1991
by South-Western Publishing Co.
Cincinnati, Ohio

ISBN: 0-538-80922-1

2 3 4 5 6 7 M 5 4 3 2 1

Printed in the United States of America

Library of Congress Cataloging-in-Publication Data

Evans, James R. (James Robert)
    Creative thinking in the decision and management sciences / James R. Evans.
        p. cm.
    Includes bibliographical references and index.
    ISBN 0-538-809221-1
    1. Creative ability in business.   2. Decision-making.
3. Management science.   I. Title.
HD53.E93   1990
658.4'03--dc20   90-47559
                                                          CIP

Gratuitous Foreword

Is is customary among academics to ask some eminent luminary in the field to write a foreword to their latest contribution to knowledge. This lends credence to the book among other academics and (dare we say) helps to promote sales. The reason for this practice is usually one of the following, none of which apply here.

The most usual reason is that the luminary is suitably ensconced at some pre-eminent institution at which the writer would also wish to be ensconced. As I teach at a school of mines with nothing even resembling a business school, this reason fails.

The next most usual reason is that the foreworder has been suitably suborned by the offer of sufficient lucre by the publisher to enthusiastically flog the book. In this case this forwarder is in a state of sufficient comfort that he has directed that whatever (lower bounded) amount the publisher would like to consider be donated to my favorite charity.

The third reason is that the writer wishes to be included in the luminary's next lucrative government research contract as a co-principal investigator. As I never do sponsored research (having the quaint notion that research should be done because it is *worth doing*), this reason also fails.

The last reason is that the luminary's name will, as mentioned above, lend academic respectability to the book. Alas, this writer *has* no academic respectability of which he is aware. My fellow academics greet my visits with all the enthusiasm that plague bacilli would greet penicillin. My job at the Colorado School of Mines has been, is, and will be to continue *to turn out the entrepreneurs of tomorrow so the socialists will have someone to tax.*

For many years now I have consulted, in my professional area, for any government agency of any country (whose politics I agree with) on a no cost basis. This is because the one thing governments seldom get from consultants is honest advice. On this basis, I may be dead wrong, but at least I have no reason to lie to them. Also, it is very important to note that, if they don't pay you, you don't have to take any nonsense-*ever*!

Simply put, my experience says that creativity is more acceptable (even to civil servants) when you obviously have no axe to grind other than the fun and opportunity to do more of your thing. Creative (off the wall) solutions sell like gang busters if they are:

1. Presented in terms the worker bees understand, and
2. If they will take the Mickey Mouse our of the work process, and
3. If they are cheaper than before.

In dealing with management, one only need remember that maximizing profit is something that only happens in textbooks of micro-economics. *An acceptable process to management is any that will perpetuate the present managment in power.*

I repeatly tell my students that there are no technical problems in this world, only technical problems hidden in psychological, behavioral, and *political* problems. The real requirement for creativity is *not* in technology, *the need for the most creativity is in getting acceptance.* In short, the right answer, (creative or uncreative) *unaccepted*, is the *wrong* answer.

In the words of the book of Ecclesiastes: "Let us hear the conclusion of the whole matter." I like Evans, I like his book, *I* think it's worth it.

Gene Woolsey, Ph.D. & all that
Professor:
The Colorado School of Mines
Adjunct or Visiting Professor:
United States Military Academy, West Point
University of Colorado Graduate School of Business
University of Waterloo, Waterloo, Ontario, Canada
Universidad Anahuac, Mexico City, Mexico
University of the Witwatersrand, Johannesburgh, RSA
Instituto Technologico De Monterrey, Monterrey, N.L., Mexico

Preface

Creative thinking is a subject that has largely been ignored in the business and engineering curricula, and almost totally ignored in the quantitative disciplines. Yet, the successful application of management science techniques to important business and engineering problems often depends on a high degree of creativity. Creative thinking also is an important attribute for any graduate student or young professor contemplating serious research.

This book is aimed at several audiences:

1. upper-level undergraduate or master's students in the decision and management sciences—including operations research, operations management, information systems, other functional areas of business such as marketing research, and related engineering disciplines such as industrial engineering—who will soon tackle that entry-level job and seek the corner office and a BMW;
2. doctoral students and young professors in these disciplines for whom BMWs are probably out of reach, but for whom research and publication are necessities; and
3. last but not least, the practitioners of the profession (with or without a BMW) who may be facing a midlife crisis and for whom intellectual curiosity and its satisfaction are their own reward.

The goals of this book are to develop in each of these audiences an awareness of creative thinking and how it can improve one's problem-solving abilities. For doctoral students and professors, I have devoted a special chapter to applying creative thinking principles to further develop and identify research ideas.

In preparing this book, I was motivated immensely by reading the many truly creative applications of the decision and management sciences in the journal *Interfaces* over the years. Many examples from this journal are cited in this book. If you are a student and are not aware of *Interfaces*, ask your professor. If he or she doesn't know what it is, go to your dean and get him or her *fired*. If any practitioner readers among you don't know what it is, for goodness sake, don't tell anyone—but get to the library *posthaste*.

Each chapter has many endnotes. *Please read them*! They provide additional references, comments, and asides on various topics. (They may be the most valuable part of this book.)

I am indebted to Harvey Brightman of Georgia State University for inviting me to write this book, to John McKinney of the University of Cincinnati for introducing me to the subject many years ago, to my colleagues Heiner Mueller-Merbach (Universität Kaiserslautern) and Gerald Smith (University of Minnesota) for their helpful suggestions and comments, and to the following individuals for their assistance in reviewing the manuscript:

John C. Anderson   Gene Woolsey
University of Minnesota   Colorado School of Mines

Roger Volkema
American University

The writings of Arthur VanGundy have had profound influence on my perspective on creative thinking. A special "hats off" to Gene Woolsey for bringing a true sense of creativity to the profession. My hope is that this book will spawn more like him (though not literally). I hope that you find this subject as fascinating as I have.

James R. Evans
University of Cincinnati

Contents

CHAPTER 1
Creativity and the Decision and Management Sciences

INTRODUCTION

Creativity is the ability to discover new relationships, to look at subjects from new perspectives, and to form new combinations from two or more concepts already in the mind. Every creation is a new combination of ideas, products, colors, textures, words, and so on. Creativity results in scientific discoveries, innovative new products, art, and literature, all of which satisfy some need of mankind.

In business and engineering, creativity is often focused on the development of new products or processes. Consider the following examples.

a. SolarCare Inc. introduced a disposable towelette called SunSense, which contains a sunscreen.

b. Alex Carswell was involved in an angry phone exchange and threw a paperweight at a picture at his desk, shattering the glass (and feeling a sense of satisfaction). He developed a novelty item called the Stressball, a soft ball with circuitry that sounds like shattering glass when thrown against an object or dropped.

c. Frank Perdue, a chicken purveyor, was unhappy with hairs that remained on chickens after processing. He bought a used jet engine to blow-dry the birds so that hairs could better be removed by singeing.[1]

Each of these examples illustrates creativity. The SolarCare product is a simple example of *combining* two common products into a new product. The

1

Stressball was the result of *looking* at anger *from a new* and humorous *perspective*. Frank Perdue *perceived a unique relationship* between chickens and jet engines to improve his production process. Each idea resulted in a new combination of existing ideas that satisfied some need of its creator.

Of course, creative behavior need not result in new *products*. A student who develops a new method for solving a problem, a manager who finds a new way of motivating employees, or an engineer who discovers a new use for some computer software are other examples of creative people. Creativity is the *generation* of novel ideas; innovation is taking those novel ideas and making money with them.[2]

Creativity is spontaneous, inner-directed, and unpredictable; one cannot be creative on demand. This is clearly the case with the Stressball; were it not for a moment of anger, the product would not have been developed. It is also doubtful that the idea for SunSense arose as a result of a systematic and directed search process or that Frank Perdue *sought* to discover a new use for jet engines. Creative ideas arise from being alert to our environment or from external stimulations. They often appear as a "flash of genius," which we usually call an "Aha!" experience. Everyone has had many such experiences, and these are the results of creative thinking.

Are you creative? Before reading further, take a moment to answer this question. One major company conducted research to determine the differences between the "creative" and "noncreative" individuals in the company. Surprisingly, or perhaps not so surprisingly, the major factor that distinguished creative from noncreative individuals was that creative individuals *believed* that they were creative. Don't despair if you answered *no* to this question; you are not alone. Everyone has creative ability, but many people do not know how to be creative. The latest research suggests that people can be *taught* to be more creative. This requires an understanding of what creativity is, what prevents people from being creative, and what techniques enhance creativity.

For many years, creativity has been the subject of serious scientific research. By the 1970s, researchers were convinced that creativity was a property of the right side of the brain and that the left side of the brain controlled logical thought. Researchers now believe, however, that this simple dichotomy is misleading. Scientists have found that creativity is a result of "mental gymnastics" that engage the conscious and subconscious parts of the brain. Creativity draws upon knowledge, imagination, logic, intuition, accidental occurrences, and constructive evaluation to discover new connections between ideas and objects.

Further research has shown that creativity is a skill that can be taught and learned. Well over 100 different techniques exist for fostering creativity. Many of these will be presented in this book. In a recent study, Sidney J. Parnes, former head of the Creative Education Foundation, found that product development engineers who used two of the more popular techniques—brainstorming and thinking through analogy—developed more useful and original product ideas than other teams.[3] Being more creative can help you to become a better businessperson, better engineer, better teacher, better researcher, or a better decision scientist or management scientist.

The Decision and Management Sciences

This book is about creativity, creative thinking, and creative problem solving in the decision and management sciences. To provide a better focus, let us define what we mean by the decision and management sciences. The Decision Sciences Institute defines **decision sciences** as "the union of the quantitative and behavioral approaches to managerial decision making encompassing all the functional areas of business." These functional areas include management information systems, finance, marketing, management, accounting, operations management, and decision support processes. Quantitative approaches to decision making include statistics and operations research.

The Institute of Management Sciences defines **management science** as "the scientific discipline devoted to the analysis of complex decision problems." Management science uses the language of mathematics and the power of models to address the stable, predictable aspects of the behavior of human-machine systems. Management science focuses on helping decision makers make choices by quantitatively estimating and forecasting the implications of those choices. It is a multidisciplinary field, using any branch of science that may have knowledge or methods essential to the understanding or analysis of a particular decision. Management scientists must select the right model and collect relevant data, but they must also make sure that the model results work in the real world.

While the perspectives of these two major professional societies are somewhat different, it is easy to see the commonalities. The decision and management sciences—which we shall denote as DS/MS—are broad disciplines that are focused on solving meaningful decision problems; that apply to a variety of functional business areas as well as the public and nonprofit sectors; and that draw on both quantitative and behavioral skills in reaching a solution. Although one usually equates decision science and management science with mathematics and models, we emphasize that neither mathematics nor models are necessary to solve important managerial decision problems. In fact, truly creative solutions to problems in these disciplines often do not rely on quantitative approaches. While many of the examples and illustrations throughout this book are quantitative in nature, our primary goal is to understand creativity and how we can use it effectively to enrich the traditional problem-solving approaches that are characteristic of the DS/MS.

THE IMPORTANCE OF CREATIVITY

Life was much simpler thousands of years ago, when agriculture was the predominant focus of work. A person needed little education, and what was learned early on lasted a lifetime. The simplicity of life demanded little creativity. The industrial age resulted in significant changes in the complexity and demands of life. People required a higher level of education and more creativity to solve problems and to use the new technology that was being discovered.

We have recently moved into an age of knowledge and information. John Scully, Chairman of the Board and CEO of Apple Computer stated:

> This is a time of profound changes in which the key economic resources in the world will no longer be capital, labor, and raw materials, but rather knowledge, individual innovators, and information. Technologies which are emerging today will give us the ability to explore, convey, and create knowledge as never before.
>
> This has enormous implications for us as individuals, as well as for our [educational] institutions. . . . We have an opportunity that is given only to few generations in history. I believe that if we respond with our best creative energies, we can unleash a new Renaissance of discovery and learning.[4]

Problem solving and decision making in today's global social and business environment have become complex tasks. The uncertainty of the future, the nature of competition, and the nature of social interaction increase the difficulty of managerial decision making. Because knowledge and technology are changing rapidly, new problems with little or no precedents continually arise. Thus, one cannot rely on existing methods and approaches to solve such problems. Truly creative approaches are becoming a necessity.

We can see similar trends by examining the history of research contributions in the decision and management sciences. If one reflects on the research literature in DS/MS, one finds that much of the early work (that is, during the 1950s and 1960s) was focused on narrow, well-defined, and highly structured problems such as linear programming, integer programming, queueing systems, and so on. Research was devoted to developing better models and more efficient solution techniques for solving these models. The research efforts of this era provided the models and solution techniques that are routinely used in solving problems at the operational levels of organizations today.

We are focusing increased research attention on broader tactical and strategic issues that integrate, both vertically and horizontally, various managerial decision problems. These problems are not as well structured as those found at the operational levels of an organization. Thus, they must be addressed more creatively.

These observations are confirmed by a Delphi study designed to determine the talents that will be required for effective leadership in the advancing global age.[5] The study suggests that creativity is perceived by representative segments of society to be a top priority for effective leadership in the global future. The author of the study states:

> Attention by educational and business communities to the development of creative potential and problem solving talents needs to accelerate. Individuals benefit in the form of more satisfying, productive, entrepreneurial lives. Groups and organizations discover creative teamwork. States and nations can likewise move from absolute nationalism to an awareness of the interconnectedness of the global family and the need to practice the arts and strategies of creative leadership.

The Need for Creativity in the Decision and Management Sciences

The practice of DS/MS must keep pace with these trends. Criticism has periodically been leveled at the failure of quantitative approaches to meet the needs of business and industry adequately. Often, the reasons for failure have been behavioral in nature; for this reason, significant research into the implementation process has been carried out. Focusing on implementation, however, presumes that the problem definition, analysis, modeling, and solution phases of a DS/MS project have been adequately performed. One can easily hypothesize that among the reasons for implementation failure is the lack of creative problem-solving abilities by the analyst.

Problem solving in DS/MS is both a science and an art. Much has been written about the *science* of decision making. This perspective typically is focused on logical, systematic, and linear ways of thinking. The literature abounds with mathematical models and solution algorithms. Courses in management science are devoted principally to the study of models and algorithms. On the other hand, relatively little has been written about the *art* of problem solving using these tools. One reason, we believe, involves a lack of understanding about creativity. J.P. Guilford stated:

> . . . problem solving and creative thinking are closely related . . . creative thinking produces novel outcomes, and problem solving involves producing a new response to a new situation, which is a novel outcome. Thus we can say that problem solving has creative aspects.[6]

Art, by its very nature, is a creative discipline. It is intuitive, haphazard, and unstructured. Russell Ackoff, one of the leading authorities in DS/MS, stated some time ago that creativity is the most important attribute of good management. Creativity is also the essence of research innovation. While creativity is strongly allied to problem solving, it has largely been ignored as a powerful component of problem solving in DS/MS. As early as 1959, Thomas Saaty noted the importance of creativity in operations research.[7] Likewise, in 1973, Muller-Merbach observed that "many operations researchers do not know much about the creative process, are not aware of how to initiate creative processes, and have no experience with the methods of stimulating creativity."[8]

As Ackoff and one of his students pointed out, creativity is

> a subject that does not fall into one disciplinary domain. Nevertheless, most of the attention it has received has come from psychologists. Decision scientists have generally ignored it. This is a pity. They have a great deal to gain from any knowledge or understanding that can enhance their client's and their own creativity. Moreover, they are in a unique position to experiment with problem solving and planning in the real world.[9]

Creativity, Productivity, and Competitiveness

Since the 1970s productivity and global competition have received significant attention both from within organizations and on a national level in the United States. This has been a direct result of the significant productivity increases realized by nations such as Japan and West Germany, as well as the overall declining rate of productivity improvement in the United States. While U.S. technology may be better than many other countries, we are struggling to compete with foreign manufacturers. Much of the success of foreign manufacturers is attributable to their creatively adapting our technological discoveries into successful and marketable products.

Thus, creativity is linked closely to productivity and competitive success in business organizations. One of the leading firms in the United States, Minnesota Mining & Manufacturing (3M), is often cited as a prime example of a company with the ability to foster a creative atmosphere among its employees. *Business Week* relates the following story:[10]

> It was 1922. Minnesota Mining & Manufacturing inventor Francis G. Okie was dreaming up ways to boost sales of sandpaper, then the company's premiere product, when a novel thought struck him. Why not sell sandpaper to men as a replacement for razor blades? Why would they risk the nicks of a sharp instrument when they could rub their cheeks smooth instead?
>
> The idea never caught on, of course. The surprise is that Okie, who continued to sand his own face, could champion such a patently wacky scheme and keep his job. But unlike most companies then—or now—3M Co. demonstrated a wide tolerance for new ideas, believing that unfettered creative thinking would pay off in the end.

Eventually, Okie developed a waterproof sandpaper that became a huge success in the automobile industry. 3M continues to develop new products faster and better than just about anyone, from Post-it™ notes to heart-lung machines. Among the reasons for its success are the ability to provide a work atmosphere conducive to creativity—with appropriate incentives and rewards— and training in techniques of creative thinking.

Organized corporate efforts to teach creativity date back to 1937, when General Electric started a two-year creative engineering program. The Creative Education Foundation of Buffalo, New York, was founded in 1954 specifically to teach creativity. Many major firms now offer in-house programs on creativity training or send their employees to off-site training seminars and workshops. In fact, more than half the Fortune 500 companies have adopted some form of creativity training. According to *Business Week*, these initiatives are paying off.[11] General Electric dishwashers now sport self-diagnostic systems that were developed in creativity sessions. Mead Corporation says that such training is helping to speed its new carbonless copy paper from the laboratory to the market. The head of management training and development at Arco Petroleum Products stated, "There's a tremendous amount of potential in our work force that we've never systematically tapped into before." This potential can be realized through better creativity.

Our educational system is a prime culprit in stifling creativity. We are too often focused on technical training and learning tools—this is the primary focus of professional education in business and engineering, for example. The process of developing one's creativity is seldom emphasized in any technical course. Nevertheless, the successful use of tools requires creative ability. It is creative thinking that truly advances a field of study and leads to significant productivity advances that provide competitive advantage.

In the next chapter we will focus on problem solving, primarily from a DS/MS perspective. This discussion will provide a foundation for later discussions of *creative* problem solving.

EXERCISES

(Exercises labeled with an asterisk are more appropriate for graduate students.)

1. Weekly news magazines routinely report on new products. Prepare a list of at least ten new products or ideas like the SolarCare and Stressball examples discussed in this chapter. Can the products or ideas on your list rightly be called *creative*? Why or why not?

*2. Select a few papers from the TIMS Franz Edleman Award Papers published in a special annual issue of *Interfaces*. Discuss the creative implications of the approaches discussed in these papers.

3. Does creativity differ between the arts and business or engineering? If so, how? You might wish to examine how education differs in these

disciplines. For example, what are the differences between curriculum and pedagogy in these disciplines?

4.   Without reading forward in this book, prepare a list of personal characteristics that you believe creative people might have. Justify your reasons for including each characteristic.

ENDNOTES

1.   The SolarCare and Stressball examples were reported in *Insight* magazine, "Having a Ball at Throwing a Fit" May 29, 1989; the story of Frank Perdue is related by Tom Peters and Nancy Austin in their book, *A Passion for Excellence* (New York: Random House, 1985) and often mentioned in their public lectures.

2.   Attributed to Robert Rosenfeld of Kodak; cited in Jack Gordon and Ron Zemke, "Making Them More Creative," *Training*, May 1986, pp. 30–45.

3.   Emily T. Smith, "Are You Creative?" *Business Week*, September 30, 1985, p. 82.

4.   Scully's statements were made in a speech delivered at the EDUCOM '87 Conference in Los Angeles on October 28, 1987, and reproduced in "The Relationship Between Business and Higher Education: A Perspective on the Twenty-First Century," *Academic Computing* (November 1987): pp. 26–29; 63–64.

5.   Berenice D. Bleedorn, "Creativity: Number One Leadership Talent For Global Futures," *The Journal of Creative Behavior* 20, no. 4 (1986): pp. 276–82.

6.   J.P. Guilford, *Way Beyond the IQ* (Buffalo, NY: Creative Education Foundation, 1977), p. 161.

7.   Thomas L. Saaty, "Some Thoughts on Creativity," Chapter 12 of *Mathematical Methods of Operations Research* (New York: McGraw-Hill, 1959). This is a very unusual (i.e., creative) chapter for a book on mathematics and, unfortunately, it lay hidden in the literature for many years.

8.   Heiner Muller-Merbach, "The Role of Creativity in the OR Approaches to Actual Problem Solving," (Paper delivered at the First International Research Conference on Operations Research, Chester, UK, September 6, 1973).

9.   Russell L. Ackoff and Elsa Vergara, "Creativity in Problem Solving and Planning: A Review," *European Journal of Operational Research* 7 (1981): pp. 1–13.

10.   Russell Mitchell, "Masters of Innovation," *Business Week*, April 10, 1989, p. 58.

11.   Emily T. Smith, "Are You Creative?" *Business Week*, September 30, 1985, p. 81.

CHAPTER 2
Problem Solving - A Basis for Creative Thinking

INTRODUCTION

We are all faced with problems at one time or another. A **problem** is a confusing or troublesome situation. Problems may be personal, economic, social, or technological. Problem solving is often considered the process of adapting to life and society. We give some typical examples of problems below.

a. A college senior has several job offers. One is in the same city as the university; the student will not have to move or build new friendships. Other jobs offer higher salaries and the chance to experience new environments and cultures. The industries also are different. A poor choice can lock the student into one industry, with difficulty in moving to a new job in the future.

b. A graduate student faces a problem in choosing a thesis topic. He or she may be interested in several different topic areas and have several different professors with whom to work closely. The choice of a topic will almost certainly direct his or her life for several years; choosing the wrong topic can lead to frustration, unhappiness, lost time and opportunity, and even failure.

c. A junior analyst in a management science department is faced with building a quantitative model for a plant's manufacturing planning system. The analyst can make several assumptions and choose many different models. The model can be structured as a linear program, a network flow model, or a dynamic program. The company has a general-purpose linear programming package on its mainframe computer. An alternative is to buy a computer code for the network model, which runs on a microcomputer. No general-purpose dynamic programming package is available; if this model is chosen, one must be written by the analyst. The choice of the wrong approach may lead to considerable user frustration and lost competitive opportunity.

Many people suggest that problems should be viewed as challenges and opportunities, not as struggles or difficulties. A positive attitude toward problem solving can increase one's success in solving problems. Creative thinking can enhance one's positive attitude by removing discouragement in problem solving. Creative thinking, therefore, is vital to successful problem solving.

All problems consist of two major elements. First, *alternate courses of action are available from which to choose, and some doubt exists as to which course of action should be selected.* Clearly, if only one course of action exists or can be viably selected, the question is moot. Also, a problem does not exist when there is no discernible difference in outcomes associated with any of the potential courses of action. Second, *there must be a need to solve the problem;* that is, the choice of a course of action can have a significant effect on the future. The need for solving a problem must belong to some individual or group that, in a sense, "owns" (is responsible for solving) the problem. This provides motivation for the problem solver, for otherwise the problem disappears. For instance, the sonic booms created by the Concorde over land may represent a problem to occupants on the ground but not to the passengers and crew in the airplane. In each of the examples given above, one can see that both major elements—the uncertainty of selecting the proper course of action and a clear need to solve the problem—exist.

We spend a considerable portion of our time on problem solving, and our success depends to a great extent on the methods and approaches that we use. Studies conducted by a psychologist, J.P. Guilford, and his associates, concluded that problem solving consists of several major cognitive functions:[1]

- the ability to think rapidly of several characteristics of a given object or situation
- classifying objects or ideas
- perceiving relationships
- thinking of alternative outcomes
- listing characteristics of a goal
- producing logical solutions

Think about the mental processes that you go through when solving a problem. Do you consciously perform *all* of the above activities? You probably do not. You probably begin by thinking about various characteristics of a problem and recording the obvious facts. You might try to classify the problem into a group of problems that you have seen before. Can you perceive relationships among seemingly unrelated objects or ideas and think with analogies? Do you develop many alternatives or list characteristics of your goal or objective? Probably, you do not do so consciously. For many problems, we may rely on experience or routine procedures to determine a solution. For other problems, routine procedures are not available, and custom-tailored solutions must be developed. Most importantly, do you use a systematic approach to solve a problem?

We will spend a considerable amount of time discussing problem-solving processes and the role of creative thinking. First, however, let us provide some essential background and perspectives on problems and problem solving.

What is a Problem?

Various formal definitions of a problem have been proposed. Among these definitions are:[2]

- a felt difficulty
- a gap or obstacle to be circumvented
- dissatisfaction with a purposeful state
- a perception of a variance, or gap, between the present and some desired state of affairs
- an undesirable situation that may be solvable by some agent, although probably with some difficulty[3]

We see that collectively, these definitions suggest some sense of consciousness of or belief in an undesirable situation, a difficulty in achieving resolution, and the hope that the problem can be solved. An important dimension of a problem is *perception*; what is a problem to one person may not be a problem to another.

Harvey Brightman characterizes two groups of problems: **disturbance problems** and **entrepreneurial problems**.[4] Disturbance problems involve removing disturbing influences by returning to where we were or are supposed to be. The gap is represented by the difference between the normal state of affairs and the state resulting from the disturbance. Such problems often arise from the failure of a system to meet its objectives as a result of poor performance or performance not directed toward the objectives. Entrepreneurial problems involve closing a gap between the present and a higher level of performance. This gap might result from the recognition that the system is meeting inappropriate objectives or that the environment has changed.

A good example of this dichotomy is found in quality assurance. The goal of production is to produce output of consistent quality that meets technical specifications. Unfortunately, every production process contains many sources of variation. Factors affecting variation include materials, tools, operators, production methods, machines, the environment, and the inspection and measurement process. The complex interaction of these factors is called the **common causes** of variation. Common causes are stable and can be described rather accurately using probability distributions. When an external effect causes the variation to drift from the stable distribution determined by common causes, it is called a **special cause** of variation. Examples of special causes would be a bad batch of materials, a machine that falls out of adjustment, or miscalibration of a measuring instrument.

Special causes are analogous to disturbance problems; they must be identified and removed in order for the process to be brought back to a stable state (called **in statistical control** in quality assurance terminology). Common causes represent entrepreneurial problems; to produce more consistent quality, they must be reduced through some improvement in technology, resulting in a higher level of performance.

THE PROBLEM-SOLVING PROCESS

Decision making is the selection of a course of action from among several alternatives. The person(s) responsible for this selection is (are) called the **decision maker(s)**. Decision makers obtain a **solution** to a problem whenever the present and desired states of affairs are perceived to be sufficiently close. Hence the size of the "gap" must be measurable, and the skills and resources needed to solve the problem must be obtainable. **Problem solving** is the activity associated with selecting an appropriate course of action and changing the present to the desired state. We cannot obtain a solution to a problem unless some change in reality or perception occurs.

Herbert Simon proposes a three-stage approach to problem solving: **intelligence, design,** and **choice**. Intelligence means recognizing the problem and analyzing problem information to develop a useful problem definition; design means generating solutions; and choice involves the selection and implementation of a solution. We view problem solving in slightly more detail. Problem solving consists of four major phases: **definition, analysis, solution,** and **implementation**. In this section we review this process, primarily from the traditional DS/MS perspective. Later in this book we shall broaden the scope of the problem-solving process when we introduce the *creative* problem-solving process.

Defining Problems[5]

Using our accepted definition of a problem as a gap between the present and some desired state of affairs, we can further define a problem by characterizing these states. The present state is usually described by what the decision maker knows about the problem. The desired state is described as a target or goal that the decision maker wants to achieve.

For many problems, the present and desired states are easy to characterize. For example, the traveling salesman problem can be described as follows. A salesman wants to visit each of n cities exactly once and return to his starting point with minimum total distance. We are given only the distances between cities. The desired state is to have a sequence of cities to visit such that the total distance travelled is the minimum. Such a problem can be stated very concisely and is clearly well defined. Most disturbance problems fall into this group.

A related problem is to find an algorithm for solving the traveling salesman problem in the shortest amount of computer time. While the present state is clearly known (we do not have such an algorithm), the desired state is clearly unknown (we do not know what such an algorithm would look like or even if it exists). Many practical problems fall into this category. For example, we know that a problem exists with dwindling oil reserves, but can we sufficiently characterize the desired state of affairs? These are examples of entrepreneurial problems.

We may also conceive of problems in which the desired state is well-defined but the present state is not well known. For example, it may be clear that we wish to reduce inventory costs, but we do not know the factors and issues that are causing excessive costs. In other problems, we may not have sufficient information about either the present or the desired states of affairs; there is only a "feeling" that something is wrong.

We summarize these different levels of problem knowledge in Figure 2-1. Useful problem definitions are those in cell 1, for the less one knows about the problem, the more difficult it will be to solve it. Since many problems initially are found in the remaining cells, we must use techniques to *move* problems into cell 1. We accomplish this by gathering and analyzing information and by redefining the initial problem statement. We shall see that structured, creative problem-solving approaches help to provide the means for doing this.

In traditional DS/MS methodology, a problem is defined by five components: the decision maker, controllable variables, uncontrollable variables, constraints, and outcomes. The **decision maker** is the person who faces the

Figure 2-1 Levels of Problem Knowledge

		Desired state	
		Known	Unknown
Present state	Known	1	2
	Unknown	3	4

problem. **Controllable variables** are those aspects of a problem situation that are under the decision maker's control. **Uncontrollable variables** are those that are not under the control of the decision maker, but which can affect the outcome of a decision. Uncontrollable variables are seldom known until after the decision has been made. **Constraints** are limitations or requirements imposed on the possible values of the variables. Finally, **outcomes** are the joint result of the decision maker's choice and the true values of the uncontrollable variables. The **value of an outcome** is a specified relationship between the controllable and uncontrollable variables. The objective that the decision maker faces is to maximize or minimize the value of the outcome.

To illustrate these concepts, consider the training of groups of employees such as airline flight attendants. Due to turnover, employees leave at a constant rate over time. The decision problem involves determining the number of employees to train in each group and the timing of the training sessions. If the group is too large, then employees will be underutilized and excess costs will be incurred. On the other hand, if the group is too small, then the training courses must be repeated very often and additional training costs will be realized.

The decision variables in this example are the number of trainees in each session and the frequency of the sessions. Uncontrollable variables include the demand for trained employees over the planning horizon, the length of time required for training, and the various costs involved. Constraints might take the form of the maximum class size allowed. The decision criterion might be specified by the objective of minimizing total relevant costs.

Problem definition is not a trivial task. The complexity of a problem increases when

- the number of potential courses of action is large,
- the problem belongs to a group rather than an individual,
- the problem solver has several competing objectives,
- the environmental conditions in which the problem occurs change rapidly,
- external groups or individuals are affected by the problem,
- the problem solver and the true owner of the problem are not the same, and
- time limitations become important.

Such issues are characteristic of problems faced in the real world. As the complexity of a problem increases, defining the problem becomes more difficult, and more creativity is needed to develop a useful problem definition.

Analyzing Problems

Analyzing problems involves sorting out and examining relevant facts and information from irrelevant ones, as well as building appropriate conceptual or mathematical models. One method of problem analysis that often assists the problem-solving effort is **classification**. Classifying problems or parts of problems helps to clarify their underlying structure and hasten the process of solving the problem. Classification can often aid in capturing past experience that will stimulate imagination and more creative solutions.

Many different schemes exist for classifying problems, both in general and in DS/MS. One of the simplest schemes, proposed by Herbert Simon, is to classify problems as well structured, semistructured, or ill-structured.[6] This is determined by the amount of information available about the gap between the present and desired state of affairs. For **well-structured problems**, we have complete information about the problem and the means of closing the gap. Such problems are usually routine and repetitive, and they can be solved by ready-made solution techniques (algorithms). It is usually easy for the problem solver to recognize which algorithm to use. A simple transportation problem is one example. We know supplies, demands, and transportation costs and seek to determine the best transportation routes to minimize total cost. We can develop a simple linear program to model this problem, and a variety of computer packages exist that will find an optimal solution. Very little creativity is needed to solve well-structured problems.

Ill-structured problems fall in the other extreme. They are characterized by a lack of good information about the problem and fuzziness about the present as well as desired state of affairs. Thus, they tend to fall into cell 4 in Figure 2-1. In addition, little or no information is available on how to solve the problem. One often "muddles through" a solution. Many public policy problems fall into this category. Such problems are so complex that complete information can never be obtained about them. In addition, human behavior is erratic and unpredictable, and alternatives cannot be listed in a simple fashion. A high degree of creativity is needed to address such problems.

Semistructured problems fall somewhere between well-structured and ill-structured problems. There is some information available to define the problem partially, but enough uncertainty exists about the actual or desired states to prevent the use of routine procedures. In Figure 2-1, problems in cells 2 and 3 usually are classified as semistructured. We often use heuristics (or rules of thumb) since our present or desired state of affairs is not sufficiently known. The design of a production facility is one example. While hard data on production rates, costs, demand, productivity, and so on can be obtained, and while mathematical or simulation models can be developed that reasonably model the system, alternatives are often not easy to specify. They need to be discovered by trial and error through extensive experimentation or analysis. Most practical problems in DS/MS usually fall within this category. While creativity is often not as important as good analytical and engineering reasoning, creative thinking can often aid the solution process and lead to solutions or solution methods that would not normally be considered.

We should note that the degree to which a problem can be classified as well-structured, semistructured, or ill-structured depends on the problem solver. The classification, in a sense, is in the eye of the beholder. Depending on one's background and experience, one individual might view a problem as highly structured while another might have no idea what to do and view it as unstructured.

Another classification scheme is proposed by Samuel Eilon.[7] He classifies decision-making problems in two dimensions, frequency and replication, and their implications for automating the decisions. The frequency with which a given decision has to be made within a given space of time is a measure of the repetitiveness of the task. Production scheduling problems, for instance, must often be solved on a daily basis, while facility location problems might be solved only once every few years. Replication refers to the uniformity in the definition of the problem. The greater the variations, the lower the level of replication. For example, all production scheduling problems within the same facility will be similar; only the individual customer orders will differ. Each facility location problem, on the other hand, will probably have many unique characteristics that depend on the nature of the facility under consideration.

Problems with a high degree of frequency and replication are generally well structured and lend themselves to programmable, automated decision procedures. Such would be the case with production scheduling or economic order-quantity decisions. Those with low frequency but high replication are still well structured and suggest the need for programmable decisions, but an economic issue exists as to whether the cost savings or other benefits justify the effort and expense involved in developing an automated procedure. The layout of equipment in a factory would fall into this category. Problems with low replication but high frequency are generally ill-structured, perhaps with many unpredictable and poorly defined characteristics and unclear objectives. Yet the high frequency suggests that decision support systems are appropriate. Student advising and the configuration of computer systems to meet individual customers' needs would be examples in this category. Finally, those problems with low replication and low frequency are the least amenable to automated decision aids. Investing in highly automated manufacturing systems is an example. Such problems are the prime candidates for creative problem-solving approaches.

Problem analysis in DS/MS typically culminates in a model; in fact, many decision and management scientists equate problem definition and analysis with modeling. This is a restricted viewpoint, because formal modeling is only one of many approaches to problem solving. However, modeling is central to many DS/MS problems, and classification schemes can also provide a useful frame of reference for modelers.

A classification scheme proposed by Russell Ackoff and Maurice Sasieni extended the Simon classification.[8] Problems in DS/MS can be classified according to the difficulty of modeling. Ackoff and Sasieni propose five categories:

1. problems in which the logical structure is simple and transparent enough to be solved by inspection and discussion

2. problems in which the structure is apparent but the way to represent it symbolically is not clear
3. problems in which the structure is not apparent but there is the possibility of extracting structure by data analysis
4. problems in which it is not possible to isolate the effects of individual variables, so we must experiment
5. problems in which sufficient data are not available, so we cannot experiment

It is easy to see that one moves from well-structured to ill-structured problems with this classfication system.

An early problem classification scheme with a model focus was given by Ackoff and Rivett.[9] They isolate seven types of problems:

1. queueing problems
2. inventory problems
3. allocation problems
4. scheduling and routing problems
5. replacement and maintenance problems
6. search problems
7. competition problems

While this classification was a valuable means of providing an early taxonomy of problems in DS/MS, it does not have enough detail to provide useful insights to model builders.

A more detailed model classification scheme is shown in Figure 2-2.[10] Models are classified by function, structure, dimensionality, temporal reference, degree of certainty, degree of generality, degree of closure, and degree of quantification. (We shall see later that such schemes can help in the creative thinking process by providing a framework for generating alternatives. This will become particularly important in the last chapter, which research topic identification.)

Gerald Nadler cautions that most classification schemes have serious deficiencies[11]. Among these are the following:

1. How does one decide where a particular problem fits within a classification scheme? As we noted earlier, classification is often in the eye of the beholder. Intuition is the best answer at the present time.
2. Few classification schemes point to a specific problem-solving approach. Little prescriptive understanding of what to do with a problem is given. Classification schemes are descriptive at best. For example, even though we stated that well-structured problems can be solved by routine algorithmic solution procedures, no guidance is suggested as to what type of approach to consider.
3. Those classification schemes leading to analytical techniques (such as the Ackoff-Rivett classification) promote deterministic thinking and limit the size of the solution space that will be explored. This

Figure 2-2 Model Classifications

Function — descriptive
          — predictive
          — normative

Structure — iconic
          — analog
          — symbolic

Dimensionality — two-dimensional
               — multidimensional

Degree of Certainty — certainty
                    — conflict
                    — risk
                    — uncertainty

Temporal Reference — static
                   — dynamic

Degree of Generality — specialized
                     — general

Degree of Closure — closed
                  — open

Degree of Quantification — Qualitative — mental
                                       — verbal
                         — Quantitative — statistical
                                        — optimization
                                        — heuristic
                                        — simulation

has been one of the major criticisms of quantitative approaches, namely, that one can become obsessed with finding a quantitative solution to the point that simple, creative solutions are overlooked. For instance, a problem of long lines at a service facility might routinely suggest a queueing approach to change the facilities while ignoring important behavioral solutions. An actual case involved complaints about long waiting times for luggage at an airport terminal. A DS/MS analyst would probably begin to look for a "technical" solution—for example, designing a new handling system to speed up delivery of baggage to the claim area. Is this what first came to your mind? The actual solution was to move the baggage claim area *further away* from the arrival gates. Passengers had to travel longer to the claim area; the baggage arrived "sooner," and the complaints disappeared.

4. Most classification schemes have a partitioning perspective, which fosters the view that working on one or more smaller problems is most effective because the whole problem is too messy to quantify.

In reality, a broad understanding of a problem is needed before trying to find solutions. Many problems, for example, cannot be pigeon-holed into a fixed classification scheme like the ones presented earlier.

These deficiencies strongly suggest that different perspectives on problems are needed. Other authors make similar observations[12], notably that:

- The application of analytic aids to organizational problems often is too easy and simplistic and is an example of a technique in search of solutions.
- Recent events might make a particular problem type obsolete.
- In some reported applications, management scientists may have biased the manager's perception of the problem and in so doing provided an inappropriate problem formulation and, ultimately, an incorrect solution.
- This type of approach is probably better suited to well-structured than ill-structured problems, since it relies on the recognition of familiar problem patterns and the presence or absence of key problem variables.

These inadequacies increase the likelihood of working on the wrong problem, restrict the solution space within which to operate during problem solving, emphasize problem details rather than resolution methods, and ignore the purposes humans seek to achieve. We observe that the above inadequacies of classification are precisely the ones that are directly addressed by the creative problem-solving approaches we shall discuss. Despite the deficiencies, problem classification is often a useful first step in helping the process of reasoning by analogy, even though it may "anchor" the decision maker's thinking. Analogical thinking is an important foundation of creative thinking. Go back and reread the example of employee training. Can you discover an analogy with a well-known problem in DS/MS? (If not, see Exercise 13 for some hints!)

Solving Problems

The definition of a problem that we have adopted leads simplistically to solving a problem: Develop the appropriate rules or transformations for closing the gap (that is, moving) between the present and desired states of affairs. However, we generally have little knowledge about how to accomplish this. If we did, problem solving would not be such an arduous task! Thus, every problem generates a new problem, namely, how to solve the original problem.

Ackoff suggests that problems can be solved, dissolved, or resolved. To **solve** a problem implies some sort of optimization. Ackoff refers to this as the "research approach," which is characteristic of traditional DS/MS modeling methodology. To **resolve** a problem, the "clinical approach," is to select a course of action that "satisfices," that is, satisfies and suffices. This process consists chiefly of trial and error, judgment, and common sense. Heuristics also play an important role, particularly when the problem cannot be formally modeled or when a model is too complex to optimize.

To illustrate this clinical approach, we shall discuss the problem of scheduling umpires for major league baseball.[13] For many years, the author has scheduled umpire crews for the American Baseball League. The problem is to assign crews to each baseball series over the course of a season to meet various scheduling constraints (such as having at least one day off when traveling from a West Coast city to Chicago or any Eastern Division city, not traveling after a night game to a daytime game the next day, and so on) and to meet two major objectives. These objectives are achieving low travel costs and balancing the number of assignments made between any given crew and team. From a formal technical perspective, we can model the problem as a very large integer program. For many reasons, however, an optimization approach is not practical. First, the problem is too large to be solved using any available computer code. Second, the nature of the costs involved is not significant enough to require fine-tuning the solution to save an extra percent or two. Third, all that the client (the Supervisor of Umpires) wants is a workable solution that will satisfy all constituents—the umpires, managers and owners, and the League President. Intelligent judgment gathered over the years has led to acceptable solutions reasonably quickly.

Finally, to **dissolve** a problem, we change the nature of the problem and/or the environment to remove the problem. Ackoff refers to this as the "design approach" and observes that it employs techniques of both the clinical and research perspectives. It involves an assessment of the total system rather than suboptimization of its parts. One example is the problem of designing a new device to pick tomatoes to reduce damage during harvesting. Although much thinking went into the mechanical design with little success, the actual solution was to develop a new tomato plant with tougher skin. Notice the similarity of this situation to the baggage-claim waiting problem presented earlier. In both cases, we dissolved the problem.

The more structured a problem is, the more likely that the research, or algorithmic, approach will be an effective means for solving the problem. While one must have a sound knowledge base of techniques and a basic facility for developing mathematical models, little creativity is required to develop a model and obtain a solution.

Most practical DS/MS applications occur for semistructured problems. The design of production and service operations (such as umpire scheduling) are typical applications that are often modeled as linear programs, simulations, and so forth. Heuristics often play an important role in the solution of such problems. In contrast to structured problems, an excellent opportunity exists for applying creative problem-solving techniques. For example, a given problem can often be modeled (for example, a linear program versus a network model) and/or solved (for example, branch-and-bound versus dynamic programming or a heuristic procedure) in a variety of ways. The resolution of these issues requires not only more technical knowledge, but also more creativity than for structured problems. We shall devote more discussion to these issues in a later chapter.

Ill-structured problems are the most difficult to analyze and solve. Often there is insufficient information even to propose an adequate model or determine a method of solution. Such problems lend themselves well to creative problem-solving approaches.[14] However, Ackoff notes that such problems are often attacked by a clinical approach due to lack of proper information about the problem, lack of time for thorough analysis, or the lack of a good problem-solving methodology.

Implementing Solutions

Implementing solutions is the final phase of the problem-solving process. Planning is the key element of implementation. Planning should include a consideration of barriers to implementation, action steps for implementing an idea, and the consequences of each step. To this end, creative thinking is vitally important.

Arthur VanGundy, a leading author in the creativity field, suggests several questions that should be considered for successful implementation.[15] These are:

1. Are resources adequate for implementing this idea?
2. Do others have the motivation and commitment needed for successful implementation?
3. Is the idea likely to meet with "closed thinking" and/or resistance to change in general?
4. Are there procedural obstacles that need to be overcome?
5. Are there structural obstacles in the organization (for example, communication channels) that need to be overcome?
6. What organizational or managerial policies will need to be overcome?
7. How much risk taking is likely to be tolerated by those responsible for implementation?
8. Are there any power struggles within the organization that might block implementation?
9. Are there any interpersonal conflicts that might prevent or hinder the idea from being put into action?
10. Is the general climate of the organization one of cooperation or distrust?

Difficulties in Problem Solving

Many problems are not adequately solved because of the lack of an appropriate methodology for problem solving and because of psychological perceptions on the part of the problem solver. Watson presents an excellent discussion of some of these issues.[16] The major difficulties in problem solving can be grouped into several categories.

1. *Failure to recognize the existence of a problem*
   a.   Some people personalize problems; that is, they may feel that a problem is a result of their own failings and thus try to hide it or ignore its existence.
   b.   Information is not received to signal that a problem exists. Subordinates often hide information from their superiors, or appropriate communication does not exist.
   c.   The problem is too complex for the perceiver to comprehend. An inexperienced manager may not understand the complexities and subtleties of a large corporate operation and therefore may not recognize certain problems.
   d.   Problems arise in contexts with which people have had no experience. In unfamiliar contexts, people may not recognize a problem. How many readers would have recognized the problem with atmospheric ozone depletion?
   e.   There is a lack of objectives or standards. Without these, one cannot separate the "present" from the "desired" state of affairs.
2. *Failure to define the correct problem*
   a.   One situation may contain many intertwined problems. It is easy to focus on the most obvious problems rather than the most important ones.
   b.   Obvious problems are often the symptoms of much deeper problems. Solutions to symptoms of problems do not necessarily remove their underlying causes.
   c.   An inability to identify accurately what is going on can lead to inaccurate problem identification. Poor information or data can easily lead to incorrect conclusions.
   d.   Incorrect inferences can lead to inaccurate problem identification. Even if data and information are accurate, inferences drawn from them may not be. Thus, strong logic is an important element of problem identification.
   e.   Poor questions yielding useless or erroneous information mislead problem solvers. Problem solvers require good detective skills to diagnose a problem situation.
   f.   Attitudes and beliefs can blind the problem solver to the real causes of an undesirable situation. Preconceptions and biases can cause the real problems to be overlooked.
   g.   Problems and their causes are oversimplified. People often lack the persistence to dig deep enough in the search for problems and true causes.
   h.   Culprits, not causes, are identified as the source of the problem.

People often seek others to blame rather than try to uncover the reasons for a problem.

i.   Accepting others' definitions leads to solving the wrong problem.
j.   All problems are often treated as logical problems. This is clear in the baggage-claim example discussed earlier in this chapter.

3. *Failure to use all available information*
   a.   The problem solver fails to seek information. Not enough time is spent on data collection and understanding the problem.
   b.   Perceptual blocks to thinking exist. Some people believe there is only one way to do things and thus have a very limited scope. They are uncomfortable with uncertainty or fear failure.
   c.   Memory limitations block the problem-solving process. Psychologists have shown that the number of items that can be held in short term memory is seven plus or minus two. In addition, the brain is not a parallel processor; it can work best at only one task at a time.

4. *Failure to recognize or question assumptions*
   a.   It is assumed that a solution to every problem exists. A problem solver can become stuck in a fruitless effort to solve an unsolvable problem and turn it into an obsession.
   b.   Rigid thinking limits one's viewpoint. A classic example is the nine dot puzzle (Figure 3-2). The objective is to cross out all nine dots with three straight lines without lifting the pencil from the paper. If one assumes *a priori* that the lines cannot extend out of the box formed by the outer dots, a solution will never be found.

5. *Failure to consider a wide range of alternatives*
   a.   Problem definition is limited. An inadequate problem definition often leads to an inadequate solution. Problems should be *redefined* from many different perspectives. Such a process often leads to unique solutions, as we saw in the tomato-picking example.
   b.   Premature evaluation or judgment takes place. Ideas are often quickly rejected because they seem silly or useless.
   c.   "Lack of time" is cited as an excuse (clinical approach).

6. *Failure to address implementation issues*
   a.   Responsibility for implementation is not determined. The list of implementation questions cited earlier in this chapter should be considered early in the problem-solving process.
   b.   There exist cultural value differences. This is true not only among societies and nations, but among and within organizations. "Corporate culture" often specifies what is acceptable or not, and deviations from the norm are often not looked upon favorably. An individual who has transferred from an atmosphere of creative freedom and support for innovative ideas to one with

      rigid structure and protocols might have an extremely difficult time implementing his or her ideas.

c. Recommendations are made instead of decisions. Volumes of reports sit on managers' shelves and are never implemented. Often this occurs when an outside consultant is used and the owner of the problem is not actively involved in the problem-solving process.

d. Solutions are not checked against the problem definition. Careless errors are made when an elegant solution simply does not make sense relative to the actual problem definition. In the worst case, the wrong solution is implemented.

e. The cost of solving a problem is greater than the benefits derived. Thus the solution never gets implemented.

Improving Problem Solving
Through Creative Thinking

The categories of problem-solving difficulties discussed in the previous section provide important clues to how we can improve our problem-solving abilities. We must develop the ability to—

1. become more sensitive to the existence of problems
2. be able to define the correct problem from possible problems among an intertwined "mess"
3. be able to seek and use all available information about a problem
4. be able to recognize and question assumptions, either explicit or implicit
5. consider a wide range of alternative problem definitions and solution ideas
6. address implementation issues early in the problem-solving process

These are precisely the goals of creative thinking enhancement.

Creative thinking will help one to improve the quality and effectiveness of problem solving and the resulting decisions that are made. Summers and White conclude that creative problem-solving techniques will also—

• reduce problem uncertainty by increasing the amount of relevant information available to the problem solver
• increase the number of potential alternatives that are generated and thus improve the chances of finding a very good solution
• increase competitive advantage by producing more unusual solutions (refer to the discussion of the 3M Company)
• decrease the number of revisions once a solution has been implemented, thus conserving critical resources
• provide for more efficient use of individual skills and abilities, thus improving morale and the organizational climate[17]

EXERCISES

1. Write down five problems that you now face and five that you resolved in the recent past. Do these meet the criteria stated in the chapter for a **problem**? How did you solve these problems? Can you write down in detail the steps that you performed?

*2. Peruse the titles of articles published in academic journals such as *Management Science* and *Decision Sciences* over the past 20 to 30 years. Can you see trends that show that the nature of problems addressed has become less narrow and more focused on broad managerial issues? Give examples and explain your conclusions.

*3. Contrast the development of computer technology with the findings of Exercise 2. How have computer technology developments helped the growth of DS/MS?

4. Develop a list of disturbance problems and entrepreneurial problems that you currently face. Can you clearly define the present and desired states of affairs? How do you measure the "gap" between them?

5. How would you classify the following problems?[18]
    a. How effectively have the marketing program and the personnel hired for implementing it performed in its two years of existence?
    b. What number of observations should be made in an activity sampling study of nurses in the hospital's surgery units?
    c. What specifications are needed for a manufacturing plant expansion of 40 percent that is supposed to meet the increased sales requirements?

6. List several problems that fall into each category of Eilon's classification scheme.

7. List several problem that fall into each category of Ackoff and Sasieni's classification scheme.

8. Using Figure 2-2, how would you classify each of the following models?
    a. linear programming
    b. a road map
    c. financial statement
    d. decision tree
    e. organizational chart
    f. PERT/CPM network
    g. simulation model
    h. breakeven analysis
    i. control chart
    j. regression model

   k. queueing model
   l. forecasting model
   m. EOQ model
   n. a model of athletic competition
   o. Markov chain
   p. plant layout

9. Provide examples of mental and verbal models.

10. For the flight attendant training program example, let

  Q = number of trainees in each session
  A = fixed cost of each training session
  C = salary paid to each trained employee
  D = annual demand for trained employees

  Construct a model to determine Q and minimize the cost of training. Can you see the analogy with a well-known DS/MS problem now?

11. Can you provide other examples like the tomato-picking or baggage-claim example in which the problem was dissolved?

ENDNOTES

1. See, for example, J.P. Guilford, *The Nature of Human Intelligence* (New York: McGraw-Hill, 1967); J.P. Guilford and R. Hoepfner, *The Analysis of Intelligence* (New York: McGraw-Hill, 1971); and P.R. Merrifield, J.P. Guilford, P.R. Christensen, and J.W. Frick, "The Role of Intellectual Factors in Problem Solving; *Psychological Monographs* 10 (1962): p. 76.

2. These definitions come from, respectively (and in chronological order), J. Dewey, *How We Think* (New York, D.C. Heath, 1933); K. Koffka, *Principles of Gestalt Psychology* (New York: Harcourt, Brace, 1935); R.L. Ackoff and F. Emery, *On Purposeful Systems* (Chicago: Aldine-Atherton, 1972); and E.M. Bartee, "A Holistic View of Problem Solving," *Management Science* 20, no. 4, Part I (1973): pp. 439–48.

3. This definition comes from Gene P. Agre, "The Concept of a Problem," *Educational Studies* 13 (1982): pp. 121–42. This paper presents a very complete conceptual development of the term.

4. Harvey J. Brightman, *Group Problem Solving: An Improved Managerial Approach* (Atlanta, GA: Business Publishing Division, Georgia State University, 1988).

5. Two good reviews of problem structuring (a term often used in lieu of problem definition) are R.N. Woolley and M. Pidd, "Problem Structuring—A Literature Review," *Journal of the Operational Research Society* 32 (1981): pp. 197–206, and Gerald F. Smith, "Towards a Heuristic Theory of Problem Structuring," *Management Science* 34 (1988): pp. 1489–1506.

6.   Herbert A. Simon, *The New Science of Management* (New York: Harper and Row, 1960).

7.   Samuel Eilon, "Structuring Unstructured Decisions," *OMEGA, International Journal of Management Science* 13, no. 5 (1985): pp. 369–77.

8.   Russell L. Ackoff and Maurice W. Sasieni, *Fundamentals of Operations Research* (New York: John Wiley & Sons, 1967).

9.   B.H.P. Rivett and R.L. Ackoff, *A Manager's Guide to O.R.* (New York: John Wiley & Sons, 1963).

10. Figure 2-2 is adapted from Richard J. Tersine and Edward T. Grasso, "Models: A Structure for Managerial Decision Making," *Industrial Management* 21 (March-April, 1979): pp. 6–11.

11. Gerald Nadler, "Human Purposeful Activities for Classifying Management Problems," *OMEGA, The International Journal of Management Science* 11, no. 1 (1983): pp. 15–26.

12. See for example, Charles Schwenk and Howard Thomas, "Formulating the Mess: The Role of Decision Aids in Problem Formulation," *OMEGA, The International Journal of Management Science* 11, no. 3 (1983): pp. 239–52.

13. For a more complete discussion of this problem and related sports scheduling problems, see James R. Evans, "Telling Umpires Where to Go: Computer-Based Scheduling for the American Baseball League," *Interfaces* 18, no. 6 (1988): pp. 42–51, and James R. Evans, John A. Hebert, and Richard F. Deckro, "Play Ball! The Scheduling of Sports Officials," *Perspectives in Computing* 4, no. 1 (1984): p. 18–29.

14. Numerous examples of creative solutions to ill-structured problems in the DS/MS field can be found in R.L. Ackoff, *The Art of Problem Solving* (New York: John Wiley & Sons, 1978) and in the many anecdotes of Gene Woolsey in the journal *Interfaces*. The reader is strongly encouraged to read and reflect on Woolsey's messages in conjunction with this book.

15. Arthur B. VanGundy, *Techniques of Structured Problem Solving* (New York: Van Nostrand Reinhold, 1981).

16. C.E. Watson, "The Problems of Problem Solving," *Business Horizons* 19 (August, 1976): pp. 88-94.

17. J. Summers and D.E. White, "Creativity Techniques: 'Toward Improvement of the Decision Process,'" *Academy of Management Review* 1 (1976): pp. 99–107.

18. Adapted from Nadler, "Human Purposeful Activities."

CHAPTER 3
Understanding Creativity

INTRODUCTION

In Chapter 1 we provided a brief introduction to creativity, focusing primarily on its importance in problem solving in the decision and management sciences. In this chapter we will delve into the subject of creativity in more depth. Our goal is to understand better the nature of creativity, the personal characteristics that lead to creativity in individuals, the barriers that prevent one from being creative, and the organizational climates that are conducive to creative behavior.

As a subject of research and formal investigation, creativity is relatively new. One of the first books on the subject, C. Spearman's *Creative Mind* (New York: D. Appleton), was published in 1931. Spearman defined creativity thus: "The power of the human mind to create new content—by transferring relations and thereby generating new 'correlates'—extends its sphere not only to representation in ideas, but also to fully sensuous presentations" (p. 148). Fortunately, current definitions are easier to comprehend.

A famous psychologist, J.P. Guilford, is credited with sparking the contemporary interest in creativity. During his 1950 presidential address to the American Psychological Association, Guilford noted that less than 0.2 percent of the literature in psychology was devoted to creativity. Since then, many books and articles have been written on creativity. Parnes et al. list almost 2000 books published from 1950–77 alone.[1] Many more books and articles have appeared since that time. It would not be possible or even desirable to try to review all the pertinent literature in the field, most of which is found in psychology and the arts. Rather, in this chapter we shall focus on many of the important themes that hold special relevance to DS/MS. Before we embark on the subject of creativity itself, however, we shall discuss some important aspects of the human mind. It is in thought that creative ideas are born.

LEARNING, THINKING, AND MEMORY

Creative insights are often the result of an "Aha!" experience—that is, a connection of thoughts living in our unconscious mind that seems to happen accidentally or serendipitously. Many years ago it was thought that this was the only way that creative ideas were born and that the conscious mind did not play a significant role. While such experiences are not usually the result of conscious thought, recent research has shown that creativity can be *facilitated* through conscious thinking. Therefore, some discussion of the inner workings of the mind can provide a better foundation for understanding creative behavior.

Let us first discuss learning. An interesting perspective on learning is that an individual progresses through four levels of knowledge:

1. unconscious incompetence
2. conscious incompetence
3. conscious competence
4. unconscious competence

For example, as a young child just learning about numbers, you had probably learned simple concepts of addition with single-digit numbers but were not aware of how to add larger numbers that required carry-over operations (unconscious incompetence). In the early grades, you became aware of your inability to perform this task (conscious incompetence). As you learned the technique, it seemed painstakingly slow, particularly because you had to "think" carefully and remember to carry digits when appropriate (conscious competence). Eventually, you reached the stage of unconscious competence, in which simple addition became second nature. But then you were in a state of unconscious incompetence about algebra!

As we learn, we continually cycle through these four stages of knowledge. A mathematics professor once told me that one studies more difficult (and apparently useless) subjects in order to make the "less difficult" (and useful) ones seem easy. The key point is that you cannot learn a subject like mathematics (or tying your shoes, for that matter) unconsciously; you must attack it in a conscious manner. The same holds for creativity. To be unconsciously competent in a creative sense, you must progress through each of the previous stages. In this chapter we will try to get you through that consciously incompetent stage!

Conscious Thinking

Cognitive psychologists are continually discovering more about the human mind, and the field of artificial intelligence tries to put these results to good use in DS/MS. Most of this study, however, focuses on **conscious thinking**. Conscious thinking uses both sensory and memory inputs. That is, information gained through our senses is processed with knowledge stored in memory to result in a concept that is meaningful to us. As an information-processing entity, conscious thinking is serial in nature and can deal with only one topic at a time, much like a (single-processor) computer. For instance, we generally read words one at a time and add numbers one digit at a time. We may switch back and forth quickly, but we cannot do both tasks simultaneously. Recent advances in computing revolve around parallel processing—the ability to perform different sets of computations independently and with coordination. Unfortunately, conscious thought does not have such capability. Furthermore, conscious thinking is quite slow.

Conscious thinking is affected by how the human brain functions and by its limitations. Psychologists have theorized that memory is divided into two components: short-term and long-term memory. Short-term memory holds information for a short time and is severely limited. If you look up an unfamiliar seven-digit phone number in a phone book, you can probably remember it long enough to make the call. If the line is busy, how many times do you have to look up the number again? Read the following number to yourself, close your eyes, and repeat it:

2 7 4 5 9 2 0

If the number also includes an area code, you probably find it more difficult to remember for a short time. Repeat the exercise with the following:

8 2 0 5 1 0 2 5 7 1

Now suppose that you also need a three-digit access code to make the call. Try the exercise once again:

4 1 9 4 7 2 8 0 0 3 5 6 1

More difficult, right? It is commonly accepted that the number of items that can be held in short-term memory is seven plus or minus two. It is easier to remember longer items of information by "chunking" or grouping the digits. Try this one:

3 6 4 A Z K 6 1 2 W E B N

This exercise is easier since the chunks are more readily identifiable, even though it is the same length as the previous example. This is why it is easy to remember long-distance phone numbers using three sets of numbers rather than trying to remember one long string.

Without looking back, can you still remember the first number? You probably cannot. Short-term memory is also limited in time, and you had no reason to save the number in long-term memory. We need some reason to retain the information. We are more likely to remember information that is related to that already in our memories and related to our experiences. For example, I find it quite easy to recall specific journal articles and approximate dates of publication related to my research interests, even if it has been many years since I referenced them. However, I am often embarrassed when forgetting the names of students I taught only the previous academic quarter.

Unconscious Thinking

Unconscious thinking represents the second important part of our mind. The unconscious mind is more difficult to understand or explain; yet it is an integral part of the creative process. In problem solving, we filter information, generate ideas, and make decisions often without direct conscious control. The unconscious mind appears to work in a nonsequential fashion and at a much faster rate than the conscious mind. We generally are not aware of such happenings. It is through the unconscious combination of ideas stored in long-term memory that the creative "Aha!" ideas are generated.

The celebrated mathematician, Jacques Hadamard, stated the role of the unconscious as follows:

> Indeed, it is obvious that invention or discovery, be it in mathematics, or anywhere else, takes place by combining ideas. Now, there is an extremely great number of such combinations, most of which are devoid of interest, while, on the contrary, very few of them can be fruitful. Which ones does our mind—I mean our conscious mind—perceive? Only the fruitful ones, or exceptionally, some which could be fruitful.
>
> However, to find these, it has been necessary to construct the very numerous possible combinations, among which the useful ones can be found.
>
> It cannot be avoided that this first operation take place, to a certain extent, at random, so that the role of chance is hardly doubtful in this first step of the mental process. But we see that that intervention of chance occurs inside the unconscious; for most of these combinations—more exactly, all those which are useless—remain unknown to us.
>
> Moreover, this shows us again the manifold character of the unconscious, which is necessary to construct those numerous combinations and to compare them with each other.[2]

Hadamard's observations provide an important clue to improving creativity: We need ways of constructing the many possible **combinations of ideas** from which we may find the useful ones. If we can provide greater conscious control over these unconscious activities, then we just might be able to improve our creative abilities. This, indeed, is the foundation of contemporary studies in creativity.

Edward DeBono proposed similar concepts of thinking and creativity in defining **vertical** and **lateral thinking**.[3] Vertical thinking develops and uses existing ideas; lateral thinking discovers new ideas. As DeBono suggests, "Vertical thinking is concerned with digging the same hole deeper. Lateral thinking is concerned with digging the hole somewhere else." Table 3-1 lists some of the significant differences between vertical and lateral thinking.

PERSPECTIVES ON CREATIVITY

As can be expected, no universally accepted definition of creativity exists. In Chapter 1 we defined creativity quite simply as

> the ability to discover new relationships, to look at subjects from new perspectives, and to form new combinations from two or more concepts already in the mind.

It is useful to examine briefly the many other perspectives from which creativity has been studied.

Definitional Viewpoints

Creativity has been defined from the viewpoints of

1. the **product** of creative behavior, such as inventions, theories, literature, music, art, algorithms, and models;
2. the **process** of creative behavior, which involves perception, thinking, learning, and motivation;

Table 3-1 Vertical vs. Lateral Thinking

Vertical Thinking	Lateral Thinking
Is a sequential process with logical progression stepwise to a solution	Is haphazard in nature and jumps around, developing its approach from the eventual solution
Selects a single best approach	Generates many alternative approaches and solutions
Avoids external influences	Actively seeks disruption
Conforms to established patterns	B r e a k s d o w n established patterns

3. **characteristics of the individual** who creates, such as temperament, personal attitudes, and habits;
4. **environmental and cultural influences** that affect creative behavior; and finally,
5. the role of creative thinking in **problem solving**.

Let us discuss each of these in turn.

A creative product, when first appearing in the mind, is new and unique *to the discoverer*. Many creative products lead to new problems, which require new solutions, which in turn lead to new discoveries. A product of creative behavior must be novel or unusual. Often, a creative product unifies much information and expresses it in a highly condensed form. Many famous scientific theories, such as $F = ma$ or $E = mc^2$ are the results of creative synthesis of information.

The process of creative behavior is concerned with the ability to transform or find new and unexpected relations among pieces of information. The **creative process** has been defined as

> that mental process in which past experience is combined and recombined, frequently with some distortion, in such a fashion that one comes up with new patterns, new configurations, new arrangements, that better solve some need of mankind.[4]

Many individuals have described their processes of creative behavior. In 1926, Wallas suggested four stages in problem solving: preparation, incubation, illumination, and verification.[5] In the preparation stage, the elements of the problem are carefully studied to learn as much as possible about it. Preliminary attempts at solution are usually carried out at this stage. If the problem is complex enough, however, the problem solver often reaches a dead end. Incubation is a period in which the problem solver turns to other tasks to let the unconscious mind churn away at all the information that has been assimilated. Illumination is the point when the solution becomes evident (aha!). Finally, verification involves testing and evaluating the proposed solution by considering its feasibility and acceptability.

Creativity does not come from sudden inspirations alone but from much hard work and labor. (Have you ever felt that you could create something that would make people say, "How creative!" but simply let it pass?) Recognizing this, normative models of creative behavior, which not only describe *how* problem solving has been observed, but also present *ways in which to do it*, have been proposed. (After all, just *how* does one incubate?) Such normative models will be the subject of a later chapter.

Psychologists have performed considerable research on the creative personality, specifically, on the characteristics that creative individuals appear to possess. The enhancement of creativity is often focused on developing these characteristics through exercises and practice. Techniques for enhancing creativity dominate popular books on the subject today.

Related to the creative personality is the creative climate. The creative climate consists of those external influences that facilitate and stimulate creativity or that hinder it. Research has identified various environmental factors that are both favorable and unfavorable to creativity. This stream of investigation is especially relevant to managers of technical personnel, such as engineers and scientists in research and development laboratories. It is also especially relevant to educators and graduate students.

Problem formulation and problem solving have been important themes in creativity research; indeed, it is the focus of this book. Ackoff and Vergara define **creativity in problem solving and planning** as

> the ability of a subject in a choice situation to modify self-imposed constraints so as to enable him to select courses of action or produce outcomes that he would not otherwise select or produce, and are more efficient or valuable to him than any he would otherwise have chosen.[6]

The first step in creative activity is often discovering and formulating the problem itself. Thus, much research in creativity is devoted to problem recognition and reformulation. A good problem formulation often leads to a simple solution.

Regardless of the particular definition or perspective adopted, several key themes stand out. Creative behavior is oriented toward solving **meaningful problems**. Creative ideas must be **useful**; lacking this attribute, they are only **original**. Usefulness, however, is time-dependent. Creativity occurs when a novel idea is made useful at some point in time. A good example of this is the development of Post-it™ note pads at the 3M Company by Arthur Fry, a 3M chemical engineer.[7] Spencer Silver, a 3M research scientist, discovered quite by accident an adhesive with very low sticking power. Since the purpose of glue usually is to bond objects well, 3M was unable to find any practical use for it. Fry was singing in his church choir and noticed that the little pieces of paper that he used to mark pages in the hymnal fell out every time he turned the page. As his mind wandered, he recalled the adhesive that Spencer had developed, and suddenly the idea struck him. Fry could put the adhesive to good use to solve his problem, and a creative idea was born.

Creativity results in **new ideas and discoveries**. Any definition of creativity must include the element of **novelty**. Creative ideas are new to us, even though the same idea may have been discovered by someone else in another place or time. As students and lifelong learners, we continually "rediscover the wheel." Such creative discovery is always a source of satisfaction and achievement.

Elements of Creativity

Creativity is a blending of **knowledge, imagination,** and **evaluation**. This process occurs through the **rearrangement and association of knowledge and experience in new ways.** Post-it™ notes are clearly a combination of imagination and association of unrelated objects in a new fashion. This book, in fact, through its association of creativity with the decision and management sciences, is simply a rearrangement of existing knowledge in a new way.

Creativity uses what is existing and available and changes it in unpredictable ways, producing unexpected results. One example in DS/MS can be found in George Dantzig's reminiscences on the development of linear programming.[8] Dantzig was trying to solve a planning problem for the Air Force, which was formulated as what we today call a linear program. His first avenue of inquiry was to determine if any such problem had been solved by economists. Dantzig was unsuccessful in this attempt and thus tried to develop an algorithm on his own. Dantzig's doctoral thesis was in mathematical statistics and involved a problem similar in nature to a linear program; however, the focus was on the existence of Lagrange multipliers. The geometric notions used in his thesis involved the columns rather than the rows of matrices. This geometry, an outgrowth of mathematical statistics, provided the insight for the simplex method.

Sidney Parnes, former director of the Creative Education Foundation, describes creativity in terms of sensitivity, synergy, and serendipity. **Sensitivity** involves awareness and perception to discover problems and invent solutions. Many internal consulting operations research groups have met their demise because of a lack of this attribute. Consultants must find problems and sell their services. **Synergy** is the behavior of a total system that is unpredicted by the behavior of any of the components. Synergy is often lacking in conscious thought. When two or more ideas are combined in a creative manner, the resulting idea is often significantly more useful than the individual ideas. For example, it had been known since the 1940s that the simplex method of linear programming could be interpreted in a special way for network flow problems. It wasn't until the 1970s, however, that this idea, when *combined* with efficient data structures from computer science, led to extremely fast computer codes for such problems.

Finally, **serendipity** refers to the awareness of the relevance of accidental happenings. Many important discoveries in science have been the result of serendipitious occurrences, the most famous, perhaps, being the discovery of penicillin.[9] While it has been observed that the most novel and greatest discoveries often occur by chance, it takes keen observation and a prepared mind to recognize the significance of such happenings.

While various definitions and perspectives on creativity exist, my favorite definition, which captures the essence of the word quite simply, comes from the creator of "Frank and Ed" in the Bartles and Jaymes wine cooler commercials: "Creativity is just doing what other people don't!"

Theories of Creativity

Over time, creativity has been viewed as

• divine inspiration

- a form of madness
- a highly developed form of intuition
- a manifestation of the creative force inherent in life itself
- a cosmic force central to the universe[10]

Such theories are speculative, without scientific basis, and do not explain the inner workings of the creative process. Psychology has provided the principal foundations upon which modern notions of creativity are based.[11]

Associationism was the dominant school of psychology during the nineteenth century. Associationism is based on the principle that thinking is the associating of ideas, derived from experience, according to laws of frequency, recency, and vividness. The more frequently, recently, and vividly two ideas have been connected, the more likely it is that, when one idea occurs, the other will accompany it. According to this theory, new ideas are developed from old ones through a process of trial and error. Creative thinking, then, is the activation of mental connections and continues until either the "right" combination is discovered or one gives up. Creative associations occur through association by resemblance, either directly or through a mediating idea, as in analogical thinking. Hence, the more associations a person has acquired, the more ideas will be at his or her disposal, and therefore, the more creative he or she will be.

Although the modern notion of creativity is based on association of ideas, ideas are *recombined*—often out of context from their original source—to form new ideas. Thus, creative thinking ignores established connections and creates its own. In fact, one would expect that relying on past associations would produce predictable rather than novel or original ideas.

Gestalt theory provides another explanation of creative thinking. According to this view, creative thinking is a reconstruction of gestalts, or patterns, that are structurally deficient. When one is faced with a problem, he or she grasps the problem as a whole. The dynamics of the problem, the forces and tensions within it, set up similar lines of stress within the mind. By following these lines of stress, the problem solver arrives at a solution that restores harmony to the whole problem. Throughout this process, the problem solver satisfies an inner urge to grasp a whole pattern and restore it to order. Creativity is an action that produces a new idea or insight through imagination rather than through reason or logic.

Gestalt theory adequately explains those situations in which one begins with a problem, but it fails to explain how one proceeds when part of the task is actually to find the problem. Problem finding is a critical aspect of creative thinking. Gestalt theory, then, does not account for the kind of creative thinking in which one must ask original questions not directly suggested by known facts.

Psychoanalysis has had an important influence on creativity today. Freud suggests that creativity originates in a conflict with the unconscious mind (the **id**). Sooner or later the unconscious produces a solution to this conflict. If the solution reinforces an activity intended by the conscious part of the personality (the **ego**), it will then issue in creative behavior. If it is at odds with the ego, it will either be repressed altogether or will emerge as a neurosis. Thus, the creative person and the neurotic are driven by the same force, the energy of the unconscious.

In Freudian psychoanalysis, much creative behavior, especially in the arts, is a substitute for and continuation of the play of childhood. Where the child expresses himself or herself in games and fantasies, the creative adult does so in writing, painting, music, research, and so on. This is clearest, perhaps, in the creative person's delight in playing with ideas for their own sake.

Creativity can be diminished by the anxiety with which the creator awaits the verdict of others on his or her work. According to psychoanalysis, a healthy ego requires that its creations be both communicated and accepted. The possiblity of rejection leads to the anxiety. Since anxiety is painful, people seek to avoid it.

One of the limitations of Freudian theory is that all mental states are determined by past mental states, particularly those of childhood, and that creativity is a recapitulation of childhood experiences. It is also assumed that society is fundamentally repressive toward creative behavior and self-fulfillment.

Neopsychoanalysis has modified the Freudian perspective. Creativity is viewed as the product of the preconscious rather than the unconscious mind. The preconscious mind is open to recall when the ego is relaxed. Creative thinking occurs when the ego voluntarily and temporarily withdraws from some area of the preconscious in order to control it more effectively later. The preconscious is the source of creativity because of its freedom to gather, compare, and rearrange ideas. This creative flexibility can be hindered by conscious thinking, which is conventional and associates ideas according to established connections.

One of the most influential psychologists of modern creativity theory is J.P. Guilford. Guilford views creativity as inherent in all persons and qualitatively similar at all levels. His concern is with quantitative differences. Thus, Guilford has developed systematic ways of measuring mental abilities involved in creativity. According to Guilford, the abilities of the mind fall into two main classes: a small class of memory abilities and a much larger class of thinking abilities. Thinking abilities are partitioned into three categories: cognitive, productive, and evaluative. Cognitive abilities involve the recognition and awareness of information; productive abilities use and generate new information; and evaluative abilities judge whether the outcomes are correct or meet requirements. Productive abilities consist of two kinds: convergent and divergent. Convergent thinking moves toward a determined or conventional answer. In contrast, divergent thinking moves in various directions toward no given answer. Convergent thinking focuses on a single correct solution, while divergent thinking may produce a variety of solutions.

Guilford lists several different factors under divergent thinking:

1. **word fluency**—the ability to produce rapidly words fulfilling specified symbolic requirements
2. **ideational fluency**—the ability to call up many ideas in a situation relatively free from restrictions, where quality of response is unimportant
3. **semantic spontaneous flexibility**—the ability or disposition to produce a diversity of ideas when free to do so
4. **figural spontaneous flexibility**—the tendency to perceive rapid alterations to perceived visual figures
5. **associational fluency**—the ability to produce words from a restricted area of meaning
6. **expressional fluency**—the ability to give up one perceived organization of lines to see another (e.g., the ability to find objects whose lines are concealed as parts of larger objects)
7. **symbolic adaptive flexibility**—the ability when dealing with symbolic material to restructure a problem or situation when necessary
8. **originality**—the ability or disposition to produce uncommon, remotely associated, or clever responses
9. **elaboration**—the ability to supply details to complete a given outline or skeleton form
10. **symbolic redefinition**—the ability to reorganize units in terms of their symbolic properties, assigning new use to elements
11. **semantic redefinition**—the ability to shift the function of an object, or part of an object, and to use it in a new way
12. **sensitivity to problems**—the ability to recognize that a problem does exist

These factors form the basis for modern creativity enhancement techniques.

Guilford believes that creative talents are largely outside the realm of intelligence as it is ordinarily measured and are widely distributed throughout the population. He also maintains that education as a whole has concentrated too much on convergent thinking, guiding students to find answers that society considers correct. Divergent thinking is generally discouraged outside the arts. Creativity is therefore inhibited. In fact, by using creativity tests on individuals of all ages, it has been found that creativity scores drop about 90 percent between the ages of 5 and 7, and by age 40 an individual is only about 2 percent as creative as he or she was at age 5.

Other theories exist that provide insights into creative thinking. Clearly, creativity is a complex issue that lacks a single, definitive explanation. As we proceed with our discussions of creativity, we will see how many of these theories relate to modern views of creativity.

Motivation for Creativity

Abraham Maslow's classic Hierarchy of Needs theory states that a priority ordering of human needs exists. These needs progress from basic physiological needs, safety and security needs, social activity needs, esteem and status needs, to the highest-order needs of self-realization and fulfillment. It was Maslow's contention that needs at each level would have to be satisfied before an individual would be concerned about the next higher level of needs.

Satisfaction of our needs, at any level of Maslow's hierarchy, often provides a strong motivation to be creative. Motivation might also arise from an organizational, rather than from a personal, need. The creation of weapons by cave dwellers was motivated by the needs of safety and security. Beethoven, realizing that he was growing deaf, worked harder and developed some of his greatest compositions in his later years. Howard Head, described as a "fanatic" in trying to develop metal skis, persisted for some seven years before developing an acceptable model. You can probably relate some experiences of your own in which you were possessed by an idea or problem, particularly about work, school, or a hobby.

Creativity is often motivated by an individual's or group's need to invent solutions from limited resources. Galileo is said to have used his pulse beat to measure the period of a swinging lamp in a cathedral in Pisa because of the lack of an adequate measuring instrument. The Japanese have shown remarkable creativity in developing solutions to manufacturing and quality problems. This is no wonder, given the limited natural resources in Japan and the Japanese culture focused on eliminating waste and conserving every precious resource available.

Management science consultants must often invent creative solutions to business problems because of the lack of time for adequate research and development, the lack of appropriate computing hardware or software, or the fact that the client must be able to understand the solution (that is, when sophisticated approaches would be rejected). More often than not, creativity is needed to get someone to use an optimization model. Woolsey suggests (with due credit to Machiavelli) that greed, fear, and the desire for status can accomplish "wonders of efficiency even in organizations that have absolutely no desire to operate efficiently, such as state, local, and federal governments."[12] Whatever the reason, motivation is an important factor in creative efforts.

CHARACTERISTICS OF CREATIVE INDIVIDUALS

The psychological and mental attitudes that we possess help to determine our ability to be creative. Many of the theories of creativity, particularly the studies of Guilford, shed light on the characteristics of individuals that appear to enhance creativity.

The elements of creativity discussed in the previous section—sensitivity, synergy, and serendipity—all require **divergent thinking**, that is, the discovery and identification of many alternatives. For divergent thinking to be successful, one must have a solid foundation of knowledge, imagination, and evaluation. Knowledge consists of the tools and skills acquired over the years as well as the experiences gained in applying them. For the successful practice of OR/MS, this includes basic technical, mathematical, and computing skills; models and algorithms; and understanding of the modeling and problem-solving process, communication skills, and interpersonal skills. An analogy between knowledge and creativity is often made with a kaleidoscope: the more pieces there are, the more patterns can be produced. Similarly, the more knowledge you have, the more ways there are of putting the pieces of knowledge together. Thus, increasing one's knowledge base of techniques and skills is necessary for creative behavior.

Imagination is the research orientation that is devoted to forming new patterns or ideas. Knowledge alone does not guarantee creativity. Pieces of knowledge, like the pieces in the kaleidoscope, must be rearranged to form new patterns and ideas. Imagination in OR/MS must include analysis—different ways of taking a problem apart, defining variables, generating hypotheses, generating ideas for solution procedures, and so on—and synthesis—putting facts together to form objectives and constraints, creating models, and identifying behavioral implications. Finally, one must be able to evaluate ideas constructively to produce useful ones.

Many other characteristics of the individual have been found to support creative behavior. Among these are:

- awareness and sensitivity to problems
- memory
- fluency
- flexibility
- originality
- self-discipline and persistence
- adaptability
- intellectual "playfulness"
- humor
- nonconformity
- tolerance for ambiguity
- self-confidence
- skepticism
- intelligence

We shall briefly examine each of these characteristics individually.

Awareness and Problem Sensitivity

Creative people have a keen sensitivity to the environment and notice things that other people do not. Often, a lack of awareness occurs because of getting locked into thinking with set patterns. For example, what do the numbers 1, 4, 9, 16, 25, 36, 49, and 64 have in common? The usual answer is that they are the squares of successive integers from 1 to 8. However, you might also notice that every other number is even or odd. An even more creative individual might make an observation regarding the *shapes* of the numbers. Can you observe any patterns based on shapes?

Good problem solvers keep in mind that nothing is perfect and that everything can be improved upon. They learn to recognize such improvements and to ask why something is as it is. Awareness is important to a DS/MS analyst, who must be able to perceive clients' problems; clients are often not aware of types of problems that can be solved using DS/MS. A researcher likewise must perceive opportunities to expand existing knowledge; thus, this is an important trait for any graduate student in DS/MS.

Problem sensitivity is the ability to recognize that a problem exists or to cut through details and misleading facts to recognize the real problem. There is a natural tendency to jump quickly to a solution without fully understanding the true nature of a problem. DS/MS analysts often fall into this trap by trying to develop a model when a model is not necessary. Einstein noted that

> The formulation of a problem is often more essential than its solution, which may be merely a matter of mathematical or experimental skill. To raise new questions, new possibilities, to regard old questions from a new angle, requires creative imagination and marks real advance in science.[13]

An interesting example of problem sensitivity was reported by Simkin and Daniels.[14] A young master's graduate went to work in the management engineering department of a large hospital. His first project was to investigate the patient parking problem in the hospital's parking garage. The garage was filled to capacity during peak hours, and many outpatients were threatening to go elsewhere. The hospital was considering building a new $10 million garage to satisfy the unfilled demand. After collecting two weeks' worth of time-stamped tickets, this young analyst found that the arrival patterns were not as random as expected and that lengths of stay were dependent on the arrival times. Specifically, a large percentage of the garage users arrived early and stayed long, and the bunching of arrivals and departures coincided with employee shift changes. These tickets also happened to have been signed with a hospital cost-center number so that the parking fees were waived. This suggested that many of those parking in the garage were employees *who were not permitted to park there.* The problem was not a need for an additional parking structure, but rather the lack of enforcement of the parking regulations!

Memory

We have already discussed the role of memory. Most creative individuals have good memories, and a few can display remarkable powers of recall. A good long-term memory is important to creativity in order to store large amounts of information that can be combined in unusual fashions to produce creative ideas. For instance, a DS/MS analyst must be able to recall different applications for various quantitative tools or books in which a similar problem was discussed. Similarly, a graduate student researcher needs to be able to recall many facts, theorems, and literature in his or her area of research. However, one need not be the Amazing Kreskin to be creative; other traits are much more important.

Fluency

Fluency relates to the ability to generate a large number of ideas easily. The creative person can produce more ideas than the ordinary person. Why is fluency important? The reason is that the more ideas you have, the greater your chances of finding a good idea. To test your fluency, in the space below list as many possible uses as you can think of for a pencil, in exactly three minutes.

How many ideas did you write down? An average person, not trained in techniques of creative thinking, will usually only list 6 to 10. A fluent, creative thinker might list as many as 40!

Guilford defines three types of fluency: ideational, associational, and expressional fluency. These relate, respectively, to fluency of generating ideas, of making remote associations, and of calling out of memory storage items of information to fulfill certain specifications. In problem solving, one sets up a search model or models, at least implicitly, that calls for information meeting certain specifications. A fluent thinker can run through the logical possibilities or alternatives quickly. To do this well, one also requires good retention and retrieval of information—that is, a good memory.

Flexibility

Flexibility refers to the ability to generate many kinds of ideas. Flexibility implies a certain fluidity of information or lack of fixedness or rigidity. Flexibility is the basis of originality, ingenuity, and inventiveness. In problem solving this relates to the ability to try a variety of approaches to solve a problem. Flexibility was characteristic of the early operations research groups through their multidisciplinary team efforts. Since OR was not a well-defined discipline, the early OR teams consisted of mathematicians, psychologists, economists, physicists, and so on. It is no wonder that a variety of approaches—mathematical, behavioral, and economic—were proposed. Unfortunately, the perspective of the discipline has narrowed somewhat over the years.

There are two types of flexibility: flexibility in producing **classes**, and flexibility in producing **transformations**. In problem solving, we generally begin at a high level of abstraction and allow our search to roam over a broad class of possibilities. Within each class, we strive for fluency of ideas. The list-making exercise described under fluency is also often used to test one's flexibility. The classes of responses that we might find for the pencil are as a tool for writing, an object that is pointed (weapon), an object that is long and thin (make holes in the ground to plant seeds), and so on. The more flexible individual will produce more classes of responses. This provides a greater chance of finding a useful idea.

A management scientist, for example, often gets locked into thinking deterministically or restricting a solution approach to linear programming. A flexible thinker will roam among different classes of ideas: mathematical programming, stochastic models, heuristics, and so on, searching for the appropriate technique.

Flexibility of transformations involves looking at problems in new ways. One question that might be asked is how a problem can be redefined to simplify its solution. If one can revise trial attempts more readily, one may obtain better answers. For example, in developing a linear programming model, can variables be redefined to provide a more useful model or greater insight into the problem?

Originality

Originality is the ability to produce unusual ideas, solve problems in unusual ways, or use things or situations in an unusual manner. Creative

individuals produce uncommon responses, make remote associations, and produce clever responses.

One of my favorite examples of a creative and original solution to a DS/
MS problem is the "Meals on Wheels" problem discussed by Bartholdi et
al.[15] Meals on Wheels is a program that delivers prepared lunches to people
who are unable to shop or cook for themselves—in this case, in Fulton County,
Georgia. The problem involved designing routes for drivers who delivered
40–50 meals to 30–40 locations between 10 a.m. and 2 p.m. daily. The client
list changed by about 14 percent each month, so the routes had to change
often. The program subsisted on minimal funding, so even a simple computer
or additional clerical effort was not possible. A method was required that
helped the busy manager generate efficient routes from a constantly changing
list. The solution was based on the idea of a "spacefilling curve." A spacefilling
curve can be imagined to visit all points in a square (see Figure 3-1). Given
such a curve, all one needs to do is to determine the relative position of each
delivery point along the curve and to sort them. The implementation of this
algorithm consisted of a street map, a table of relative position values for the
spacefilling curve, and two Rolodex card files. The street map was mounted
under a plastic grid so that location coordinates could be easily read. The
table was used to translate the coordinates into the relative position values.
One Rolodex file was used to store the clients alphabetically, and the other
to sort the clients by relative position values. With the card files, it was easy
to add or remove clients.

Self-Discipline and Persistence

Creative individuals not only develop novel ideas, but they also work
hard and persistently to follow them up. Howard Head, as we had mentioned
earlier, sustained efforts over long periods of time and against many obstacles
in developing the first usable metal skis. A major scientific journal said that
work on an anticholesterol agent at Merck Pharmaceuticals would likely be
fruitless. Nevertheless, the company persisted, and the drug became "a potential blockbuster." Novel ideas are not always easy to implement, partic-

Figure 3-1 Example of Construction of a Spacefilling Curve

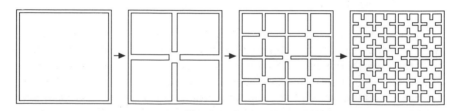

ularly with limited resources or in organizations in which the corporate culture is difficult to change. Graduate students, especially, need to be constantly reminded of this in pursuit of their research ideas.

Adaptability

Creative individuals are open to new experiences. They have wide interests and often jump from one to another rather easily. They work best when in close contact with colleagues and other individuals having different orientations and experiences. Being adaptive is important to DS/MS practitioners. Problems arising from different clients might involve statistics one day, linear programming the next, and simulation later on. Such people must relish these different opportunities and challenges and adapt to new or unfamiliar situations in the business environment.[16]

Intellectual "Playfulness"

Creative individuals like to explore ideas for their own sake. This is why many are found in academics and in research laboratories where such behavior is encouraged and rewarded. There is a close connection of this attribute with fluency. While such an attribute is clearly important to graduate students, it is equally important to practitioners. Organizations must allow their employees to experiment and, at times, to fail.

Humor

Humor is the ability to react spontaneously to discordance in meaning or implication. Humor is often the result of a "twist" in meaning of a conventional concept. A creative person sees more meanings in a situation than an ordinary person; these meanings are often subtle and unusual. In psychoanalytic terms, the ego is highly flexible and can withdraw more easily from the subconscious. This permits one to make novel connections, which is the essence of humor. Is "The Far Side" one of your favorite comic strips? Gary Larson *beams* creativity.

Nonconformity

Conformity inhibits creativity. The conformist is generally less intelligent, less flexible, and less fluent than his or her counterpart; he or she is more emotionally repressed, denies access to the creative subconscious, is less confident, lacks faith in his own ideas, seeks security and acceptance, and therefore shuns novelty. The nonconformist is less conventional and has a compulsion to be different. This willingness to be different allows him or her to take risks even if there is a chance of failure. Mistakes are often viewed as opportunities for developing better ideas. Nonconformity is often very difficult in highly structured organizations; it is easier in industrial research labs and in universities.

Tolerance of Ambiguity

A creative person actively seeks uncertainty, complexity, and disorder, both for the challenge that is presented and also for the satisfaction that will result when the situation is resolved. "Real" problems are nearly always ambiguous. DS/MS analysts, like surgeons, must often wade through rolls of fat to get at the muscle. (Note the creative analogy!)

Self-Confidence

Creative people have an inner confidence in the worth of their work and a sense of mission or destiny. Decision and management scientists as well as creative researchers must be able to work independently and without close supervision.

Skepticism

Most people are conservative, trusting what is known and mistrusting that which is not. The creative person is skeptical of accepted ideas and often plays devil's advocate, questioning facts and assumptions. Many recognized geniuses can hold on to apparent contradictions until they are no longer contradictions.[17] Part of Einstein's genius was an inability to understand the obvious. A management scientist is constantly looking for ways to improve productivity and efficiency in an organization. A researcher is always seeking a better method or theory.

Woolsey has always cautioned management scientists to be skeptical of data. While most analysts may know what to do with data, they usually do not know where it comes from, how it was collected, or how much to trust it. Woolsey's "Bean Counter Theorem" is, "Either the data is not present, or if it is present, it is not in the right form."[18]

Intelligence

Creative people have above-average intelligence but are not necessarily near the top of the scale. This, of course, depends on the type of work performed. For example, a scientist requires higher intelligence to master his or her subject than a writer or an artist. Since DS/MS depends heavily on mathematics, one must possess above-average intelligence to succeed.

While we have highlighted many of the characteristics of creative in-dividuals, we have certainly not addressed all of them. Creative people gen-erally also have good analysis and synthesis skills, often prefer the complex to the simple, have high self-esteem and personal courage, exhibit curiosity, and are impulsive. However, you should not believe that a creative person must have each of these traits. Collectively, they imply that the creative personality exhibits a certain "looseness" that permits independent and free thinking. Understanding these characteristics provides suggestions for en-hancing creativity. Strengthen them! Indeed, this is what we shall discuss in the next chapter.

BARRIERS TO CREATIVITY

Psychological research has suggested that the two halves of the brain are responsible for different types of thinking. The left brain controls judicial thought, which analyzes, compares, and chooses; the right brain is associated with creative behavior, namely, visualizing and generating ideas. Recent re-search, however, tends to refute these propositions.[19] Nevertheless, we think both judicially and creatively. This also helps to explain one of the major barriers to creativity.

Over 90 percent of formal education trains our judicial thinking. We are taught the "one correct way" to solve problems, to judge, to critique. As a result, judgment grows with age, and creativity dwindles. We must decouple judgment from imagination.

Textbooks instill judicial thinking, particularly in the quantitative dis-ciplines. For example, problems of type X are *always* modeled as linear pro-grams, while those of type Y are *always* modeled as Markov processes. Seldom are alternative modeling strategies presented.

To emphasize this point, consider the following problem, commonly found in elementary algebra texts: Jack is three times as old as Jane. Three years ago the sum of their ages was 22. How old is Jane now? Before con-tinuing, solve this problem yourself.

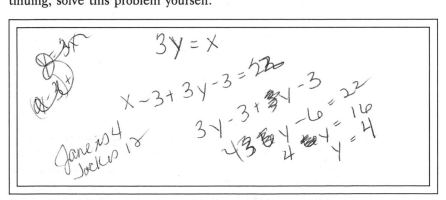

How did you do it? We suspect the most common approach (though obviously not the only one) is to let $x = $ Jack's age, $y = $ Jane's age, and solve the equations

$$y = 3x$$
$$(y - 3) + (x - 3) = 22$$

However, this problem was found in a chapter on "single-variable equations." The student is forced to view the problem as having one unknown (because simultaneous equations have not yet been introduced) and must be able to recognize indirectly and substitute $y = 3x$ into the second equation. The "correct" approach is to formulate the problem as

$$(3x - 3) + (x - 3) = 22$$

in one pass. Is it any wonder that more complex modeling and problem-solving tasks present difficulty? Ackoff relates other examples of how creativity is suppressed in primary education.[20]

The traditional educational process does not develop our abilities to recognize problems, to see remote relationships, or to distinguish between cause and effect. Our perceptions of problem solving are limited by past experiences. We become victims of habit and rigid thinking, trying to solve problems using old methods and seeking the *optimum optimorum*, or the "optimum of all optima."[21] We learn and practice sophisticated optimization methods, when all a manager often needs is an evaluation of alternative courses of action or a solution that is better than he or she now has available. The discussion of problem classification schemes in DS/MS in Chapter 2 reinforces these premises.

Creative ability does not belong to a select few who are "born with it." A fundamental premise of creative thinking is that *all* people have innate creative potential. Unfortunately, all people also have culturally produced internal and external barriers to the use of their creative ability. These barriers most often are due to habits and various blocks to creativity.

Habits

Habits are necessary to perform many of our daily activities, both personal and professional, without expending unnecessary energy. We are conditioned through education and experience in life into developing habits. We develop habits about the way we dress, eat, and play. Nearly every aspect of our physical lives is governed by habit, and habits become ingrained in our unconscious minds. However, habits can keep us confined to viewing things in a conventional way. When habits hinder creativity, we fall into a rut. To see how easily we can fall into a rut, take a piece of paper or a card and cover up the series of numbers that follows. Then, uncovering one number at a time, say it aloud and *add* it to the previous sum, keeping a cumulative total.

```
1000
  10
1000
  20
1000
  30
1000
  40
```

What is your answer?[22] Make sure you read the endnote now!

In business, corporate culture depends on habits that have been ingrained in the organization for many years. Habits such as dress codes and formal communication channels reflect conformity and security. The military, the government, and nearly every big corporation has its own corporate culture. Only in the most innovative companies is creative risk-taking encouraged or rewarded. Yet these firms are among the most successful.

As another exercise on habit, fold your arms in front of you. Now *reverse* the position of your arms. Feels strange, right? In fact, you probably had to *think* carefully to do it correctly. When bad habits arise, it takes *conscious* efforts to break them. This usually feels awkward at first. If you have ever tried to change a golf grip or a tennis swing, you know well how difficult this is.

Similar statements hold true for intellectual habits as well. Habits can be useful when we need to solve problems similar to those that we have seen before. However, with *new* problems, we tend to limit our thinking to solutions that we used in the past, which may not be appropriate. A habit is like an algorithm; it always works the same way and leads to the same conclusion.

With habits, our thinking becomes rigid; we call this **functional fixation** or **problem-solving rigidity**. Gene Woolsey relates a story of a company that had formulated a salesman allocation problem as an integer program with 1,600 variables and 400 constraints and was seeking advice on the feasibility of solving it.[23] (As a historical note, this was around 1970; ask your older professors about the computational ability of solving integer programs back then, on *mainframe* computers using punched cards!) Woolsey's response was to ask what was currently being done. He was told that two "little old ladies" had been doing this problem manually for some years. He then asked if the OR group had ever thought to study them to see what they were doing. They hadn't, and, in fact, the little old ladies were found to be performing in a near-optimal fashion. Clearly, habits such as routinely searching for the quantitative solution inhibit creativity and decision-making ability. We need to recognize the effects of habits before we can remove them and become more creative.

Creativity Blocks

James L. Adams, who has written several popular books on creativity, defines four classes of blocks to creativity: perceptual blocks, emotional blocks, cultural and environmental blocks, and intellectual and expressive blocks.[24]

Perceptual Blocks

Perceptual blocks are obstacles that prevent a problem solver from clearly perceiving either a problem itself or the information needed to solve the problem. Perceptual blocks arise in many forms. The first is stereotyping and labeling. With stereotyping, you see what you expect to see. This is the basis for "dressing for success," for instance. To develop a creative idea, you must allow a concept to assume a different role when combining it with other concepts in a unique fashion. Stereotyping makes this difficult. When a label has been applied, it is difficult to notice the true qualities of the person, concept, or object. For example, labeling linear programming as a "resource allocation" method makes it difficult to see its potential use in statistics.

A second perceptual block is difficulty in isolating the true problem. This may be because of misleading or inadequate information, because the owner of the problem is too involved in it to see it clearly, or because of functional fixation such as being too solution-minded. The airport baggage-handling problem and tomato-picker problem examples discussed in Chapter 2 provide illustrations of such perceptual blocks.

A third and very common type of perceptual block is adding artificial constraints and assumptions to a problem. You may have already seen the famous "nine-dot" problem shown in Figure 3-2. The problem is to draw no more than four straight lines, without lifting the pencil from the paper, so as to cross through all nine dots. Try it.

A common artificial constraint that many people add to this problem is not allowing the pencil to cross the boundary defined by the eight exterior dots (Figure 3-3), or assuming that the paper cannot be folded or placed on a sphere. (How would these ideas lead to a solution?) Such a perceptual block generally occurs from too limited a problem statement.

A similar problem is given in Figure 3-4. Move three sticks to form four squares. What artificial constraint would most people (or you!) put on this problem?

A fourth perceptual block is the inability to see a problem from various viewpoints. What is one half of thirteen? Write your answer(s) in the space below.

**Figure 3-2
The Nine-Dot
Problem**

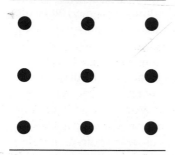

**Figure 3-3
Artificial
Constraints in the
Nine-Dot Problem**

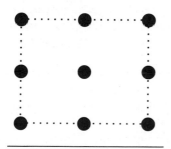

Figure 3-4 A Stick(y) Problem

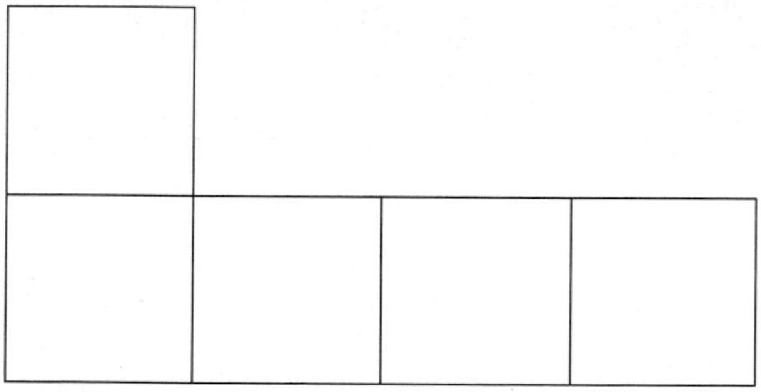

Undoubtedly, you answered 6.5. This is the "safe" answer. More creative answers are 1 and 3 (split the number 13 into its two digits); 11 and 2 (do the same for the Roman numeral representation); "thir" and "teen"; and a baker's dozen over two. These answers result from the ability to see the number 13 from alternate viewpoints.

John Mulvey provides a good example in DS/MS of viewing a problem from different perspectives.[25] The problem involved scheduling of some 100 faculty and 500 courses over three academic quarters within the Graduate School of Management at UCLA. Mulvey developed three formulations of the problem: as a network flow problem, as a detailed integer programming problem, and as an aggregation of the network model that is considerably smaller but less detailed. Each of the approaches had various advantages and disadvantages. For example, the network models were much more user-friendly to implement than the integer programming model; the integer programming model was more realistic than the others and provided more detailed information; the aggregate model required less data and less computational time to solve. Viewing the problem from three different perspectives resulted in a better evaluation of the different criteria and hence a better solution.

Robert Machol observes that people solve problems using the tools they know best.[26] Using a traffic flow example, he notes that a physicist would view automobiles as molecules in a Maxwellian gas; the electrical engineer considers it a servomechanism; the statistician as a stochastic process; and so on. How much easier it might be to solve problems if DS/MS analysts could consider other approaches suggested by physics, electrical engineering, and other disciplines.

Thomas Saaty notes, "It is not necessary to limit oneself to the field of one's academic specialty in order to tackle a problem creatively."[27] A recent winner of the Nobel Prize in economics said that he would never have been able to come up with his ideas if he had been trained as an economist. This also is evident in DS/MS when one considers the advancements made in optimization algorithms because of the use of improved data structures from computer science. More recently, simulated annealing, genetic algorithms, and neural networks have shown the importance of drawing ideas from diverse disciplines. Saturation, particularly involving data, is a common perceptual block in DS/MS. One of Gene Woolsey's classic quotes is

> If the cost of collecting the data for a model is greater than the amount you can save by solving it, *you shouldn't do that*.

Management scientists can easily become immersed in data collection without seeing the big picture. Saturation can often result in serious functional fixation. Woolsey discusses a sophisticated integer programming problem that he showed could be solved by a simple nomogram.[28] The modelers got so wrapped up in their model that they did not see alternatives for solving the problem.

Finally, the failure to use all sensory inputs often hinders problem solving. Consider the following problem.[29] In performing a physical inventory count, an individual was faced with the task of counting some thousands of coal buckets. The buckets covered a large area and were in stacks of 24. If the stacks had been arranged in regular rows, the task would have been fairly simple. As it was, the stacks were pushed together in an irregular mass. It was impossible to walk over the buckets to count the stacks, and there was no time to rehandle and restack them. How was this accomplished? The creative solution was to use *sight*; the individual took a picture of the warehouse room from a tall ladder and counted the stacks!

Emotional Blocks

Emotional blocks to creative problem solving involve the fear of making mistakes or taking risks, the inability to tolerate ambiguity, the desire for security and order, a preference for judging ideas rather than generating them, inability to relax and put the problem aside for a while, lack of challenge, overmotivation to succeed quickly, lack of imaginative control, and the inability to distinguish reality from fantasy.

Emotional blocks follow from Freudian theory—specifically, that creative thinking is inhibited by the conscious ego as discussed earlier in this chapter. Humanistic psychology leads to other conclusions:

1. A person creates for conflict resolution or self-fulfillment.
2. At least part of creativity occurs at an unconscious level.
3. Creativity is highest in the absence of neuroses.
4. The conscious mind, or ego, is a control valve for creativity.
5. Creativity can provoke anxieties.

The most common emotional block is the fear of making a mistake or taking a risk. This is a natural consequence of our educational and cultural development and relates closely to the psychoanalytic perspectives of Freud. We are afraid of looking silly or embarrassing ourselves. Such attitudes are reinforced by parents, teachers, and supervisors. In the workplace, these attitudes only stifle innovation. Many companies, such as 3M, for example, *encourage* experimentation, risk-taking, and failure—reaping the rewards when new and innovative products emerge.

As we noted earlier, education is focused on judicial thinking. Thus it is not surprising that ideas are judged, or rather *prejudged*, before they can be adequately considered on their merits. Judging ideas too early in the problem-solving process will lead to unnecessary and inappropriate rejection of many ideas. Comments such as, "That's a silly idea," "It will never work," "Too theoretical," "Too trivial," or "The best linear program is the one with the fewest constraints," are examples. Fear of making a mistake or looking foolish commonly leads to premature judgments. We seek security and tend to distrust supervisors and colleagues.

New ideas require additional information for proper judgment—hidden merits may arise after further consideration. Also, ideas lead to other ideas; by rejecting them early on, you lose this opportunity to "piggyback" on an idea that will perhaps lead to an outstanding one. Much of creative problem solving is focused on understanding this block.

Since the unconscious mind plays a crucial role in creativity, we must give it the opportunity to work. "Aha!" experiences occur *after* the unconscious has had the opportunity to churn away at the information that has been collected. This is the incubation period described by Wallas. Wanting to get an answer too quickly or procrastinating until just before a deadline does not provide sufficient time for such incubation.

Other emotional blocks include the lack of challenge and excessive zeal. We can become stuck in performing routine tasks, with no challenge to motivate to be creative. Excessive zeal also inhibits creativity. We spend too much time on details and fail to see the big picture. Woolsey and Swanson provide the example of an operations research group in an oil company that worried about the third decimal place in a linear programming output, when the data on viscosity of the input stream had been obtained by a refinery worker's rubbing it between his fingers.

Cultural and Environmental Blocks

Cultural and environmental blocks are acquired from cultural patterns and our immediate social and physical environment. Some examples of cultural blocks are that "Play is for children only," "Quantitative methods are useless" (old-time management perspective), "Qualitative methods are useless" (new-wave mathematics perspective), "Any problem can be solved given enough resources," and taboos. Environmental blocks might include an autocratic boss, distractions (such as constant meetings or phone calls), lack of time, and the lack of support to bring ideas into action.

Intellectual and Expressive Blocks

Intellectual and expressive blocks include the inefficient choice of mental tactics or a shortage of intellectual ammunition. Examples might be solving a problem using the wrong language (mathematical when a verbal solution is more appropriate), inflexible use of problem-solving strategies, lack of correct information, or inadequate language skill to express ideas.

We now see another simple and direct means of enhancing creativity: Remove these blocks!

CREATIVE CLIMATE

We have discussed those characteristics of individuals that support creative behavior and those mental blocks that hinder it. Externally, organizational climate also has a major impact on creativity. Many aspects of our external environment affect our ability to perform creatively. Procedures, policies, rewards and punishments, communication, equipment, clients, co-workers, and so on all affect our creative behavior. Creativity can be threatening to many managers. Managers often *mismanage* creativity for many reasons.[30] Among the reasons noted for a lack of creativity are:

- Many managers believe that time spent on creativity is diverted from the time available for other purposes.
- Some creative ideas and suggestions are politically unwise; thus they are resisted.
- Creative individuals are generally high turnover risks and can be lured away by other companies that desire their talents and skills. Therefore, managers will not commit to them.
- Highly creative organizations tend to be less predictable and more changeable than those emphasizing efficiency and productivity. Some managers find these conditions distressing.
- Highly creative people can be an economic burden on the company. Managers generally are evaluated on economic performance.

These are simply excuses that result from a lack of understanding about creativity. Creativity can improve the quality of solutions to organizational problems, result in economically viable innovations, and enhance personal and group effectiveness.

External factors that are conducive to creative thinking include:[31]

- *Providing freedom to do things differently, encouraging risk taking, encouraging self-initiated projects, providing assistance in developing ideas, and providing time for individual efforts.* 3M is a master at this. When an employee comes up with a new product idea, he or she recruits an action team to develop it. Salaries and promotions are tied to the product's progress, and the employee has the chance to run his or her own product group or division if the product succeeds. If an idea cannot find a home in one of 3M's existing divisions, an employee can devote 15 percent of his or her time to prove it is workable. For those who need seed money, as many as 90 Genesis grants of $50,000 are awarded each year. In a similar fashion, Hewlett-Packard allows researchers to spend 10 percent of their time on pet projects and makes labs and equipment available 24 hours a day.
- *Maintaining an optimal amount of work pressure, providing a nonpunitive environment, using a low level of supervision, providing realistic work goals.* Many internal DS/MS consulting groups must generate a certain amount of billable revenues; yet they have the freedom to select or reject their own projects. Work goals affect motivation; unrealistic goals can result in dissatisfaction and poor job performance.
- *Delegating responsibilities, providing immediate and timely feedback, demonstrating confidence in the workforce in a climate of mutual respect, allowing individuals to be part of the decision-making process.* 3M has made substantial changes in areas such as production and quality control. New manufacturing layouts place more burden on supervisors, who, for instance, are now in charge of entire product lines—such as masking tape—and not just specific functions

like slitting. Operators are expected to identify quality problems immediately and are asked for their input in how to improve the job.

- *Encouraging participation and interaction with others outside the work group.* 3M researchers, marketers, and managers visit with customers and routinely invite them to help brainstorm product ideas. General Electric also jointly develops products with customers.
- *Encouraging open expression of ideas, accepting "off the wall" ideas.* Rubbermaid, for instance, looks for fresh design ideas anywhere; one of their projects involves applying the Ford Taurus-style "soft look" to garbage cans.

In general, the culture of many organizations does not support these conditions that lead to creative behavior. Cultural change, education, and training are necessary to develop a creative climate. This discussion points to a third means of enhancing creativity: Improve the climate within which individuals work.

In the next chapter, we shall discuss how creativity can be developed using the three means presented here—namely, improving individual characteristics that support creative behavior, removing blocks to creativity, and improving organizational climate.

EXERCISES

1. Think about how you add numbers. What habits do you use? Write them down. How would you add the following numbers?

    3 6 7 4 2 5 8 5 1 6 9 4

    Do your habits help or hinder your work?

2. List five habits that you have. What prevents you from changing them?

3. Have you ever been able to develop an effective solution to a problem from new ideas once you broke past habits? Write up a case study.

4. List several "Aha!" experiences you can recall. Remember what you were doing at the time of these experiences.

5. Develop examples of exercises that would test or develop Guilford's divergent thinking factors.

6. Examine your own behavior. What characteristics of creative individuals do you believe that you possess? Provide examples that justify your response.

7. List all the landmarks that you pass on your way to work or school. Next time you travel the route, pay closer attention. Were you really aware of all of them?

8. List as many uses for the following items as you can in three minutes:
    a. popcorn
    b. toothpicks
    c. a toothbrush
    d. marbles

9. List as many different problem *types* as you can for which linear programming is useful.

10. Using the guidelines suggested for developing creativity within business organizations, suggest ways in which professors can encourage a better creative climate in the classroom.

11. Make up a short story using the following: a mouse, a box of cereal, a telephone, a computer disk, and a pair of socks.

12. Describe a school homecoming or Tournament of Roses Parade float that you would design.

13. Write down as many "opening lines" for meeting members of the opposite sex as you can think of. Analyze your list for fluency, flexibility, and originality.

14. Think of as many April Fool's jokes to play on a friend or spouse as you can.

15. A man walked into a room and found Sam and Diane lying dead on the floor. There was broken glass and water all around them. How did Sam and Diane die? (What assumptions did you make or challenge?)

16. Though I am no cartoonist, I drew upon the Far Side humor and created the following:

THE REAL REASON FOR THE EARTH'S ROTATION

Make up other "real reasons" for natural phenomena.

17. Think of ten unusual (uncommon but not disgusting) food combinations (like cottage cheese and ketchup—a favorite of one of my college buddies).

18.   Think of humorous titles for your college textbooks.

19.   Which of Guilford's divergent thinking factors are tested for in the following exercises?
      a.   List uses for a common object, such as a brick or toothpicks.
      b.   Suggest a number of objects that would be best for starting a fire.
      c.   Ask a person to list words beginning with a specified prefix, such as "con" or "pre."
      d.   Name a sport by combining the end of one word with the beginning of the next in a sentence; for example, the sentences, "I must get my guitar out of hock. Key is stuck," give the word "hockey."
      e.   List synonyms for certain words.
      f.   Name things that are white, soft, and edible.
      g.   produce words that mean the opposite of "dry."
      h.   Write different sentences, each containing three given words.

ENDNOTES

1.   Sidney J. Parnes, R.B. Noller, and A.M. Biondi, eds., *Guide to Creative Action* (New York: Charles Scribner's Sons, 1977).

2.   J. Hadamard, *The Psychology of Invention in the Mathematical Field* (Princeton, NJ: Princeton University Press, 1945).

3.   Edward DeBono, "Information Processing and New Ideas—Lateral and Vertical Thinking," in Parnes et al., *Guide to Creative Action*.

4.   J.E. Arnold, "Summer Session Notes," unpublished manuscript, Massachusetts Institute of Technology Creative Engineering Laboratory, cited in Charles S. Whiting, *Creative Thinking* (New York: Reinhold, 1958).

5.   Graham Wallas, *The Art of Thought* (New York: Harcourt Brace, 1926).

6.   Russell L. Ackoff and Elsa Vergara, "Creativity in Problem Solving and Planning: A Review," *European Journal of Operational Research* 7 (1981): pp. 1–13.

7.   "For 10 Years, Post-its Stick Around," *Insight*, January 29, 1990, p. 41.

8.   George B. Dantzig, "Reminiscences About the Origins of Linear Programming," *Operations Research Letters* 1, no. 2: pp. 43–48.

9.   Martin F. Rosenman provides a discussion of serendipity in Alexander Flemming's discovery of penicillin in "Serendipity and Scientific Discovery," *Journal of Creative Behavior* 22, no. 2 (1988): pp. 132–38.

10. Further discussion of the origins of these perspectives can be found in George F. Kneller, *The Art and Science of Creativity* (New York: Holt, Rinehart and Winston, 1965).

11. See note 9 above. The theories discussed in this section are adapted from this

work. More complete discussions can be found in Irving A. Taylor and J.W. Getzels, eds., *Perspectives in Creativity* (Chicago: Aldine Publishing Co., 1975).

12.   Robert E.D. Woolsey and Huntington S. Swanson, *Operations Research for Immediate Application: A Quick and Dirty Manual* (New York: Harper & Row, 1975), p. 66.

13.   A. Einstein and L. Infeld, *The Evolution of Physics* (New York: Simon and Schuster, 1938).

14.   Mark G. Simkin and Edward B. Daniels, "He Saved the Company $10 Million—And Apologized!" *Interfaces* 19, no. 3 (May-June 1989): pp. 61–64.

15.   John J. Bartholdi III, Loren K. Platzman, R. Lee Collins, and William H. Warden III, "A Minimal Technology Routing System for Meals on Wheels," *Interfaces* 13, no. 3 (June 1983): pp. 1–8.

16.   For a practical discussion of these issues, see Gene Woolsey, "Some Reflections on Surviving as an Internal Consultant, Azerbaijan, & Two Thieves," *Interfaces* 5, no. 1 (November 1974): pp. 48–51.

17.   See Albert Rothenberg, *The Emerging Goddess* (Chicago: University of Chicago Press, 1979), for a treatise on creativity in art, science, and other fields. This book is based on considerable empirical research.

18.   Woolsey and Swanson, *Operations Research*, p. 168. See also Gene Woolsey, "The Measure of M.S./O.R. Applications or Let's Hear It For The Bean Counters," *Interfaces* 5, no. 2 (February 1975): pp. 74–78.

19.   A good survey on this topic is Terence Hines, "Left Brain/Right Brain Mythology and Implications for Management and Training," *Academy of Management Review* 12, no. 4 (1987): pp. 600–606.

20.   Russell L. Ackoff, *The Art of Problem Solving* (New York: John Wiley & Sons, 1978). This is a delightful book focused on practical aspects of problem solving in DS/MS, with a heavy emphasis on the concepts underlying creative thinking. It is well worth reading.

21.   Robert Machol, "Principles of Operations Research, 7. The Optimum Optimorum," *Interfaces* 4, no. 4 (August 1974): pp. 52–53.

22.   Was your answer 5,000? If so, add them again! Many people fall into this habit.

23.   R.E.D. Woolsey, "A Candle to Saint Jude, or Four Real World Applications of Integer Programming," *Interfaces* 2, no. 2 (1972): p. 20–27.

24.   James L. Adams, *Conceptual Blockbusting: A Guide to Better Ideas* (New York: W.W. Norton, 1974 and subsequent revised editions). This popular book is devoted entirely to understanding and breaking blocks to creativity.

25.   John M. Mulvey, "Strategies in Modeling: A Personnel Scheduling Example," *Interfaces* 9, no. 3 (May 1979): pp. 66–76.

26.   Robert Machol, "Principles of Operations Research: The Screwdriver Syndrome," *Interfaces* 4, no. 3 (1974): pp. 26–27.

27.   Thomas L. Saaty, *Mathematical Methods of Operations Research* (New York: McGraw-Hill, 1959).

28.   Robert E.D. Woolsey, "A Novena to St. Jude, or Four Edifying Case Studies in Mathematical Programming," *Interfaces* 4, no. 1 (November 1975): pp. 32–39. Woolsey notes that a major reason for the failure of mathematical programming is that the modeler does not realize that the method is a *means* to an end rather than an end in itself.

29.   This example comes from H.N. Broyles and is adapted from Alex F. Osborn and Robert B. Wentworth, "100 Problems and Exercises for Creative Thinking," in Parnes et al., *Guide to Creative Action*.

30.   Michael K. Badawy, "How to Prevent Creativity Mismanagement," *Research Management* 29, no. 4 (July-August, 1986): p. 28.

31.   These factors are discussed further in Arthur VanGundy, *Creative Problem Solving: A Guide for Trainers and Management* (New York: Quorum Books, 1987), and in Scott G. Isaksen, "Toward a Model for the Facilitation of Creative Problem Solving," *Journal of Creative Behavior* 17, no. 1 (1983): pp. 18–31. Examples from 3M and other companies are adapted from Russell Mitchell, "Masters of Innovation: How 3M Keeps its New Products Coming," *Business Week*, April 10, 1989, pp. 58–63.

CHAPTER 4
Developing and Enhancing Creativity

INTRODUCTION

In Chapter 3 we discussed the many attributes that creative individuals have and the internal and external blocks that prevent one from being creative. We can take a variety of steps to enhance creativity.

1. We can help individuals to understand the influence of their backgrounds, experiences, and habits on behavior. In this way, individuals are allowed to perceive themselves as being creative and to remove the internal blocks to creative behavior.
2. We can create a climate to encourage creative thinking by removing external blocks to creativity. Sensitivity to problems can be increased, skills that will enhance the gathering of knowledge can be taught, methods to release imagination can be developed, and systematic means for evaluating ideas can be learned.
3. We can provide opportunities to practice creative thinking in a nonjudgmental, nonpunitive climate.

Research, particularly that carried out by Sidney J. Parnes at the Creative Education Foundation, has shown the following:

- Creative imagination can be deliberately developed.
- Creative problem-solving courses can measurably improve the ability of students of average intelligence to produce good ideas, the criteria of quality being uniqueness and usefulness.

- A systematic course of instruction in applied imagination can also produce significant gains in personality traits such as confidence, initiative, and leadership potential.

In a recent study, Basadur et al. conducted controlled field experimentation with manufacturing engineers to assess the effectiveness of creativity training on performance.[1] They concluded that such training positively affected engineers' attitudes toward divergent thinking in problem solving.

Developing and enhancing creativity focuses on improving the individual traits that support creative behavior and breaking the blocks that hinder creativity. Even though creativity occurs in the unconscious mind, we can consciously stimulate our creative juices. Henri Poincaré noted, "This unconscious work is not possible, or in any case not fruitful, unless it is first preceded and then followed by a period of conscious work."[2] Conscious methods for creativity strive to guide the formation and flow of ideas in the mind. They act as seeding vehicles to provide new insights, and they hasten the creative thinking process and help to overcome obstacles to creativity by focusing our thoughts and energies.

IMPROVING CREATIVE CHARACTERISTICS

In Chapter 3 we discussed a variety of characteristics that creative individuals seem to have in common. One way of enhancing one's creativity is to focus on improving these traits. We can enhance creativity through a wide variety of life experiences. Only by gaining knowledge from a variety of fields can one possibly make the novel connections that are the essence of creative thinking. Thus, it is important that students take a variety of courses, not just focusing on technical subjects such as business or engineering. Liberal arts, travel, jobs, and hobbies all add to our knowledge and imagination. Games and puzzles provide a rich source of activity for developing the characteristics that enhance creativity.

The two most important rules for creative thinking are to **defer judgment**, and to **produce large quantities of ideas**. These rules form the basis for brainstorming, a technique that we shall discuss later in this chapter. In general, most of us are anxious to put forth ideas and get them into action as soon as possible. We often fail to take the time to consider strange or unusual ideas that might indeed be very useful. We prematurely reject ideas that seem foolish. We can often refine and develop such ideas into useful ideas. Deferring judgment eliminates self-criticism which is the most detrimental psychological block to being creative. We must maintain a positive attitude when generating ideas.

The reason we seek large quantities of ideas is that the more ideas you have, the better they will likely be. Obviously, to produce a large quantity of ideas, you must defer judgment on the ideas that initially are found. We need to be able to separate our imagination from our judgment.

Among the most important characteristics of creativity are the ability to test assumptions (problem sensitivity), fluency, flexibility, and originality. Exercise is needed to develop our minds as well as our bodies. Many exercises, like the ones we discussed in Chapter 2, are available to expand the mind and develop these abilities.[3] Some exercises are given below; discussion of the answers can be found in the endnotes to this chapter.

Problem Sensitivity Exercises

1. Show how to cut a circle into eight pieces using only three cuts. Try it using only two cuts.[4]

2. Draw a picture of your car's dashboard.[5]

3. Select a common model in management science (for example, the transportation problem, PERT/CPM, or EOQ model). Write down all assumptions made in using the model.[6]

Fluency Exercises

To be fluent, let your mind run free and write down whatever ideas arise. Try to remove any worries or problems that you might be facing at the time. Do not prejudge any ideas; you can always come back later and evaluate them. Try using free association; that is, use one idea as a stimulus for the next. Look for idea stimulation in your immediate environment. For example, a pair of scissors on your desk might suggest cutting down the size of a problem, or a balloon might suggest expanding the number of variables in a model. Most importantly, write your ideas down (or record them on microcassette)! It is easy to forget fleeting thoughts; many creative people keep a pencil and paper beside their beds for those ideas that strike in the middle of the night.

1. In one minute, list as many words as you can that start with "re."[7]

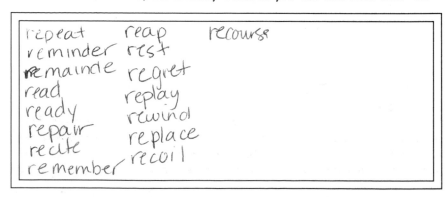

2. Write down as many five-word sentences as possible in which the first letter of the first word is F, the first letter of the second word is C, the first letter of the third word is O, the fourth begins with M, and the fifth begins with B. Your sentences need not be completely logical.[8]

FCOMB
FRank Came over Monday Barefoot
FRed can't oil my Brakes
Flies cook oatmeal mash Blindly.
forks Crash over my Bowl
~~Fluggose Coore copora~~
Feliciacan often miss baskets

3. In what ways are a PERT/CPM network and a transportation problem tableau similar? In what ways are they dissimilar?[9]

Flexibility Exercises

To improve flexibility, try different problem-solving languages. Don't get stuck with a mathematical or computer-based approach. Use visualization, analogies, and draw pictures. Many mathematical problems can be easily solved without mathematics. Woolsey relates a marvelous story on this subject.[10]

A growing city recognized a need for improving its police dispatching operations. They sought a computer system to assign squad cars to minimize the response time for calls. Not buying the "we need a computer" mindset, our creative consultant spent considerable time riding in patrol cars and learning the dispatch procedures; then he built a "dispatching computer" as follows: He drew nine vertical and nine horizontal lines on the city map roughly the same distance apart, numbering the squares. He took a carnival wheel, dividing it into 100 segments. Through each one of the pie slices, he mounted a three-inch screw so that it stuck through at least half an inch on the other side. He bought 100 small plastic boxes and drilled a hole in each side: one hole big enough to drop buckshot in and the other to screw the box to the back of the wheel. From the police call book he found the location of each call for a patrol car on the map grid, and for each one he placed a piece of buckshot in the plastic box.

When a call came in, he spun the wheel and noted the number on the plastic box at the very bottom. He located the number on the city map, read off an intersection of the map in that square, and told the squad car to go there. He then placed pins, with the number of the car that called, in the square where it was going and in the square it was coming from—and stretched a rubber band between them.

When a code three (lights-and-siren call) came in, it took only a short time to find the appropriate square number on the map, figure out which pin was closest to that square (or which car's rubber band stretched close to the area), call the car, and dispatch it. Both pins were then placed in the square where it had been sent. A piece of buckshot was placed in the box on the wheel matching the square of the call. Each month, the boxes were removed from the wheel, weighed, and arranged from heaviest to lightest. The amount of buckshot in the lightest box was removed from all boxes, and they were remounted on the wheel. This was done to prevent the wheel from being overloaded. This solution reduced the average response time by 35 percent!

Another technique to improve flexibility is to break down the problem into various pieces: parts, operations, functions, purposes, and so on, and then try to generate as many different ideas as possible for each.[11]

1. Look at Figure 4-1. What do you see?[12]

Figure 4-1
A Flexibility Exercise

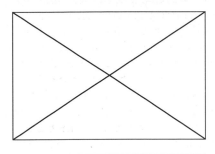

2. Find an elementary linear programming problem statement in a text-book. Discuss how you would apply computer simulation to the problem. For graduate students: how would you solve a linear program using nonlinear programming techniques?[13]

3. Consider the following problem: A product can be produced in each of T successive time periods. The demand for each time period t is D_t, the production cost is c_t, and holding cost from period t to $t + 1$ is h_t. The initial and final inventories are zero. Determine the optimal production plan for each time period. Model this problem from at least three different perspectives.[14]

Originality Exercises

To improve originality, don't overemphasize it. By trying too hard to be original, you may place too much stress on yourself. Instead, focus on generating a large quantity of ideas, and originality will follow. *Believe* that you are creative.

1. Write a short paragraph using only the words listed below, adding only verbs, prepositions, and articles.[15]

~~Ferrari~~	~~Radio~~	~~Richard Nixon~~	~~Parking lot~~	~~Giraffe~~
~~Boy~~	~~Girl~~	~~Professor~~	~~Shoes~~	~~Mustard~~
~~Ice~~	~~Mouse~~	~~Book~~	~~Computer~~	~~Tree~~
~~Diploma~~	~~Driver~~	~~Sidewalk~~	~~Teddy bear~~	~~Baby~~

Richard Nixon was driving through the parking lot in his Ferrari. ~~Florda~~ The Radio was on and a girl was sitting under a tree with mustard green shoes on ~~and~~ a Baby, with a Teddy Bear and a giraffe, was standing on the sidewalk waiting for ~~the~~ Boy ~~with~~ ~~the~~ and a Professor with a ~~Bo~~ computer to walk by. The driver, R.N, hit a mouse while ~~was~~ reading a book and watching the Baby ~~The driver braked but slid on the ice and~~ killed the boy. The boy didn't get the diploma

2. A salesman must visit 50 cities and return to the one from which he started. His goal is to minimize the total travel distance. Devise methods for finding the best possible sequence of cities to visit.[16]

TECHNIQUES FOR GENERATING IDEAS

Many techniques have been developed to help in the process of generating ideas. Ideation techniques are often divided into **individual techniques** and **group techniques**. While individual techniques can be used by groups, not all group techniques can be used by individuals. Among the most common are brainstorming, synectics, checklists, forced relationships, attribute listing, and morphological analysis.

Brainstorming

Brainstorming is one of the most popular techniques for idea generation. Brainstorming was introduced by Alex Osborn in the late 1930s. He brought the idea to the masses through his book *Applied Imagination*, first published in 1953. Brainstorming is based on the concept that we are not creative because we filter (prejudge) ideas because of the perceptual blocks that we discussed in the previous chapter. Therefore, Osborn focused on eliminating this filter. In conducting brainstorming sessions, he silenced criticism by ringing a bell loudly.

Brainstorming is based on two basic principles and four rules. The two basic principles are to **defer judgment** (rule out criticism) and that **quantity breeds quality** (strive for large quantities of ideas). The four rules are:

1. Rule out criticism. We must withhold evaluation until after ideas have been generated.
2. Welcome freewheeling. Participants are encouraged to suggest any ideas that come to mind, the wilder the better. An atmosphere is created in which all inhibitions are relaxed.
3. Seek large quantities of ideas.
4. Encourage combination and improvement. This is often called **piggybacking**, that is, combining two previous ideas or improving upon a previous idea.

Brainstorming is usually viewed as a group problem-solving technique, capitalizing on the fact that ideas from one person stimulate ideas from others, although it can be practiced on an individual basis. A brainstorming session consists of the group members, a leader, and a recording secretary. Subordinates should not be mixed with supervisors in order to avoid any environmental blocks or pressures. All group members as well as the leader should have some familiarity with the nature of the problem. The leader should be able to maintain a relaxed atmosphere and be skilled in prompting additional ideas. The purpose of the recording secretary is to write down the ideas as they are proposed.

A typical brainstorming session is performed as follows. A group of 6 to 12 participants is usually selected. The participants develop a concise problem statement. The background of the problem, examples of possible solutions, and the four brainstorming rules are sent to the participants 2–7 days prior to the session. It is important that all participants understand the problem and the process. Next, an orientation meeting is held to explain the format of how the session will be conducted, review the fundamental principles, and perform a warm-up exercise unrelated to the problem. The problem under consideration is then written on the board. Participants are requested to propose ideas. Only one idea should be suggested at a time, and the leader must maintain control over the group. The secretary should write down the ideas.

Sessions should last about 30–45 minutes. After the ideas are generated, an evaluation group of about five individuals is chosen. They are presented with the list and select the best ideas. These ideas are given to the original group by way of a report from the evaluation group, and the original group is requested to list any additional ideas.

The problem addressed with a brainstorming session should be specific rather than general, so that participants can concentrate their efforts on a single, focused topic. For example, improving quality in an organization is too broad. Such a problem must be broken down into more specific pieces, such as improving the quality of purchased parts or focusing on a specific manufacturing operation. We should use brainstorming only for problems that call for idea-finding rather than judgment. Problems with limited options, such as whether to make or buy a part, clearly are not suitable for brainstorming either.

Brainstorming works because of its synergistic effect. The number of ideas generated by several individuals is not additive; piggy-backing of others' ideas will lead to an exponential growth of ideas. Friendly competition among individuals in the group also increases motivation to be creative. Since no criticism is allowed, internal blocks to creativity are removed.

Synectics

In the early 1950s, William J.J. Gordon, an executive of Arthur D. Little, Inc. who had studied creative thinking and Osborn's theories, began tape-recording sessions of his creative team. He noticed that when a particularly novel idea emerged, it was expressed as an analogy with a similar problem found in nature or elsewhere in life. For example, when a farm products company had asked the group to help it come up with a way to ensure that seeds were properly spaced in the field, the group developed the idea of packing the seeds in a dissolvable tape that would be laid in the field. The idea arose after someone thought of a machine gun belt.[17]

Gordon began to research some of history's notable discoveries and found that analogy had been the key insight that led to the discovery in nearly all cases. Gordon formalized the process as a technique that he called **synectics**. The method involves group sessions in which a problem-solving group is led through a series of steps beginning with background information, reducing a problem to its barest essentials, and finally followed by searching for a natural analogy.

One of the most notable results was the development of Pringle's Potato chips. A company had sought to find a way to compress potato chips into a small space. Clearly, when this is done they are crushed. With synectics, the question to ask was: Had nature solved the problem? The analogy was found in leaves. Although fragile, they are often found compressed and undamaged. This is the case when they were moistened. (Have you noticed how much easier it is to rake and bag them after a rain? Have you ever tried *watering* leaves before raking them?) The company later sold the idea to Procter & Gamble, who introduced the product.

Synectics is derived from a Greek word meaning the joining together of different and apparently irrelevant elements. First, it tries to **make the familiar strange** by pulling the problem solver away from the problem so that creative solutions can be developed. Second, it tries to **make the strange familiar** by viewing the problem in a new way.

Synectics has two distinguishing characteristics. First, the group attacks the *underlying concept* of the problem rather than the problem itself. For instance, if a new principle for a can opener is sought, the group leader introduces the subject of opening. Second, the group examines the problem from many angles—economic, social, mechanical, and so on—to try to discover an analogy or metaphor.

Three basic types of analogies are used: fantasy, direct, and personal. Fantasy analogies are based on viewing a problem in terms of idealistic wishes rather than actualities. For example, man had dreamed of flying like a bird, going to the moon, or swimming like a fish for centuries. The myth of Icarus and Jules Verne's *Nautilus* may very well have given the spark of imagination to the development of airplanes and submarines. Operations researchers have often fantasized of moving directly to an optimum point of a linear program without moving among extreme points as does the simplex method. The search for ideal solutions can often lead back to practical ideas, such as the ellipsoid methods for linear programming and Karmarker's algorithm.

Direct analogy involves finding parallel situations in real life based on your own experiences and knowledge. For example, Bell developed the telephone by modeling it after the human ear. To optimize an unknown surface, we can think of hill climbing. If we are blindfolded and placed on the side of a hill, we can take one step in several directions and choose the one that moves upward the fastest. Many algorithms for nonlinear optimization are based on this analogy.

Many successful algorithms for combinatorial optimization problems are based on direct analogies. "Simulated annealing" involves an analogy with the annealing process in materials science and "genetic algorithms" are based on biological reproductive processes. *Science News* reported on April 25, 1987, that a molecular biologist and a zoologist investigating how nerve cells are linked discovered an analogy with the traveling salesman problem. They started with a small circle in the middle of the group of cities. The circle was gradually stretched out because of the forces exerted by the points until it formed an irregular loop that passed near every point, thus specifying a traveling salesman tour. They have been able to solve 100 city problems within 1 percent of optimality using this method. Taking this analogy in reverse, the scientists hope that this *algorithm* will provide new insights into neural connections.

Personal analogies involve placing yourself in the role of the problem itself. You imagine yourself as the person or object being studied. For example, product designers might place themselves in the role of the user of the product, or salespeople might place themselves in the role of the customer. Gene Woolsey relates an interesting story involving personal analogy.[18] A company had determined that substantial bottlenecks in moving paperwork for RFQs (requests for quote) through a plant existed. Formal methods of flowcharting the process and analyzing the flowchart did not seem to uncover all the problems. Here's how he attacked it:

> Tomorrow morning, when the mail comes in, meet me in the mailroom wearing an old shirt. We will then pick an RFQ at random and staple it to your shirtcollar. Now *you* are that RFQ, and you may not move from that spot until you are taken to the next place where you (the RFQ) are to be processed. Further, you may not take that RFQ *off* until you (the RFQ) have been completely processed thru the plant.

In response to the fact that they got around 40 RFQs each day, Woolsey suggested:

> ... I would show up with 40 School of Mines students wearing old shirts. We would staple the RFQs to their shirtcollars and simultaneously equip them with a case of cold Coors beer and two bags of Fritos. They would receive the same instructions as the plant manager: that they are now the RFQs and may only move to the next processing station when taken there by someone. However, they receive one further instruction that they will be supplied with beer and Fritos as fast as they consume them. Later in the afternoon, all the plant manager has to do to find bottlenecks is to go looking for *groups of drunks*.

A trained leader is essential in performing synectics; it is not a do-it-yourself method. However, the use of metaphors is an excellent idea-generation method. The use of analogies has recently been investigated by Sullivan and Yates as a tool for comprehensive business planning.[19] When considering a specific business problem, managers often find it useful to know how other companies have approached the same problem. Sullivan and Yates describe a knowledge base of cases pertaining to one business area and a support system that, given sufficient information about a company, will search the knowledge base and propose analogous cases for further management study.

Checklists

Checklists are a simple means of generating ideas by preparing a list of items related to a problem and checking the items against certain aspects of the problem. Osborn suggested a checklist approach to help generate ideas. Below we list the major questions to consider.

- *Put to other uses?* New ways to use as is? Other uses if modified?
- *Adapt?* What else is like this? What other idea does this suggest? Does the past offer a parallel? What could I copy? Whom could I emulate?
- *Modify?* New twist? Change meaning, color, motion, sound, odor, form, shape? Other changes?
- *Magnify?* What to add? More time? Greater frequency? Stronger? Higher? Longer? Thicker? Extra value? Plus ingredient? Duplicate? Multiply? Exaggerate?
- *Minify?* What to subtract? Smaller? Condensed? Miniature? Lower? Shorter? Lighter? Omit? Streamline? Split up? Understate?
- *Substitute?* Who else instead? What else instead? Other ingredient? Other material? Other process? Other power? Other place? Other approach? Other tone of voice?
- *Rearrange?* Interchange components? Other pattern? Other layout? Other sequence? Transpose cause and effect? Change pace? Change schedule?
- *Reverse?* Transpose positive and negative? How about opposites? Turn it backward? Turn it upside down? Reverse roles? Change shoes? Turn tables? Turn other cheek?

- *Combine?* How about a blend, an alloy, an assortment, an ensemble? Combine units? Combine purposes? Combine appeals? Combine ideas?

We often use such checklists for developing new product ideas.[20] For example, we can add or subtract features, change colors, substitute materials, rearrange parts, vary shapes, change size, and so on. The same checklist can be used for idea generation in DS/MS. For example:

1. Put to other uses—Apply the EOQ model to personnel planning.
2. Adapt—Adapt principles of annealing in materials science to combinatorial optimization—"simulated annealing."
3. Modify—Relax deterministic assumptions.
4. Magnify—Enlarge the number of variables in a linear program to obtain better sensitivity analysis information.[21]
5. Minify—Aggregate variables or constraints to reduce model size.
6. Substitute—Use a linear approximation for a nonlinear objective function.
7. Rearrange—Change the order of operations, such as "cluster first, route second" or "route first, cluster second" in vehicle routing applications.
8. Reverse—Use backward chaining as opposed to forward chaining in expert system search processes.
9. Combine—Utilize parallel processing.

George Polya, a celebrated mathematician particularly noted for his approach to problem solving, suggests a checklist for solving mathematical problems.[22]

Understanding the Problem. What is the unknown? What are the data? What is the condition? Is it possible to satisfy the condition? Is the condition sufficient to determine the unknown? Or is it insufficient? Or redundant? Or contradictory? Draw a figure. Introduce suitable notation. Separate the various parts of the condition. Can you write them down?

Devising a Plan. Have you seen it before? Or have you seen the same problem in a slightly different form? Do you know a related problem? Do you know a theorem that could be useful? Look at the unknown. Try to think of a familiar problem having the same or a similar unknown.

Here is a problem related to yours and solved before. Could you use it? Could you use its method? Should you introduce some auxiliary element in order to make its use possible? Could you restate the problem? Could you restate it still differently? Go back to definitions.

If you cannot solve the proposed problem, try to solve some related problem first. Could you imagine a more accessible related problem? A more general problem? A more special problem? An analogous problem? Could you solve a part of the problem? Keep only a part of the condition, drop the other part: how far is the unknown then determined, how can it vary?

Could you derive something useful from the data? Could you think of other data appropriate to determine the unknown? Could you change the unknown or the data, or both, if necessary, so that the new unknown and the new data are nearer to each other? Did you use all the data? Did you use the whole condition? Have you taken into account all essential notions involved in the problem?

Carrying Out the Plan. Carrying out your plan of the solution, check each step. Can you see clearly that the step is correct? Can you prove that it is correct?

Examining the Solution Obtained. Can you check the result? Can you check the argument? Can you derive the result differently? Can you see it at a glance? Can you use the result of the method for some other problem?

Within this list are the essential elements of creative thinking: problem sensitivity and testing assumptions (Is the condition sufficient to determine the unknown? Could you restate the problem?); flexibility (Could you restate it still differently? Draw a figure?); and analogy (Have you seen the same problem in a slightly different form? Do you know a related problem?).

Polya actually provides more than simply a checklist; he presents an overall problem-solving approach. In the next chapter, we shall see that this approach is closely related to more generic creative problem-solving approaches.

Let us consider how this list might be adapted to modeling (not solving) linear programming problems.

Understanding the Problem. What are the decision variables? What are the parameters (data)? What are the constraints? Is sufficient data available to determine all the relevant constraints? Draw a picture.[23] Introduce suitable notation. Separate the various parts of the constraint (for example, left-hand-side, right-hand-side). Write them down.

Devising a Plan. Have you seen it before? (Is it a product mix, transportation, or scheduling problem, for example?) Or have you seen the same problem in a slightly different form (different notation or different form of constraints)? Do you know a related problem? Could you restate the problem using different decision variables or a different objective function? Could you think of other data or constraints appropriate to the problem (for instance, material balance equations that are not explicit in the problem statement)? Did you use all the data?

Carrying Out The Plan. Write down each constraint. Perform a dimensional analysis of each term and both sides of the constraint. Are the dimensions consistent?

Examining the Solution Obtained. If numerical values are substituted for the decision variables, would the owner of the problem have a useful solution? When solved, does the solution make sense?

Forced Relationships

Forced relationships is a technique that helps develop the ability to generate ideas by forcing a relationship between seemingly unrelated ideas. Forced relationships is based on one of the principles of brainstorming, namely, combining and recombining ideas. Ideas do not necessarily have to be related to each other or the problem in question. However, ideas that are related to each other and to the problem will generally produce more practical ideas, although they may be more mundane. For example, consider the problem of finding a better way of training users of computer software. We might first list general items in the subject area: disk, book, computer, and so forth. Forcing *disk* and *book* together might suggest the idea of putting the users' manual on the disk. Forcing the concepts of *book* and *computer* together might suggest a computer-based instructional system, for instance.

The forced-relationship technique is extremely useful in generating research ideas in DS/MS; this will be discussed in Chapter 6.

Attribute Listing

Attribute listing involves taking specific aspects of a problem, listing their attributes, and then focusing on these attributes to generate new ideas. The attributes are used as a checklist to force the problem solver to examine all aspects of the problem. For instance, the attributes of a paper clip are that it is thin, metal, pliable, has sharp ends, and so on. To determine different uses for a paper clip, one might focus on these attributes individually. What uses can one have for a thin object—a tooth pick, a pipe cleaner? A metal object—a heating element, an electrical conductor? A pliable object—a cork screw, a fish hook? A sharp object—a weapon, a paper cutter?

In DS/MS, listing and analyzing model assumptions is an application of attribute listing. For instance, the classic EOQ model assumes a constant demand rate, no stockouts, fixed order costs, constant lead time, order quantity arriving all at once, and so on. How might each of these assumptions be changed? Demand can be stochastic, lumpy, or nonlinear. Stockouts can be included, and they can be lost sales or backorders; or only a fraction of unsatisfied demand may result in lost sales. This technique can provide a rich source of model-building enhancement.

As another example, consider the problem of snow removal on a county highway network. The major elements of the problem are the vehicle, weather conditions, routing, location of the salt depot, and so on. Attributes of the vehicle might be its size (tons of salt that it can carry) and whether or not it is equipped with a plow. We might characterize the weather conditions as light snow, medium snow, or heavy snow, and so on. By listing such attributes, it is much easier to develop alternative approaches for attacking the problem. For instance, with a light snow, one might dispatch only small trucks to salt bridges; for a heavy snow, an entire fleet plan would probably be developed.

Morphological Analysis

Morphological analysis involves the use of a grid system to examine combinations of attributes along several dimensions. In essence, it combines

principles of forced-relationship and attribute-listing techniques. Morphological analysis is based on the simple principle of combination: If there are n
elements with m attributes each, then there are m^n possible combinations of
the attributes. For example, a paper clip might have the elements of shape
(round or square), material (metal or plastic), and thickness (thick or thin).
This gives eight combinations (see Figure 4-2). We might produce a round,
plastic, thin paper clip, or a square, metal, thick one, for example.

The various combinations of attributes of EOQ model assumptions provide a variety of possible models when viewed morphologically. For instance,
considering demand (deterministic or stochastic), stockouts (none, lost sales,
backorders), order costs (fixed, dependent on order size), lead time (deterministic or stochastic), leads to $2 \times 3 \times 2 \times 2 = 24$ different models![24]

DEVELOPING A CREATIVE
CLIMATE

Creativity in industrial organizations is the result of creative people
working in a creative environment. The organizational literature contains
many different recommendations for fostering creativity. Some of these are
listed below:[25]

- *Remove or reduce obstacles to creativity within an organization.* These obstacles
  include the various environmental blocks that we discussed in Chapter 3.
  In addition, creative people should be relieved of routine duties and administrative chores.
- *Match jobs to individuals' creative abilities.* Some people are best working
  alone; others are better in groups. Some work well in 9-to-5 time frames;

**Figure 4-2 Example of
Morphological Analysis**

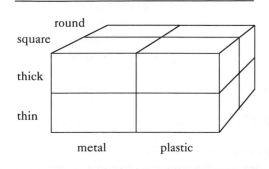

others require flex time. Managers need to be tolerant of individual idio-syncrasies, nonconformity of dress codes, frequent coffee breaks, and so on.

- *Tolerate failures and establish direction.* Creative people need an atmosphere that allows radical ideas without being harshly judged. Seemingly silly ideas often turn into the best products. However, appropriate direction must be given, and realistic goals and objectives must be set to maintain a sense of urgency.
- *Improve motivation to increase productivity and solve problems creatively.* Creative accomplishments should be recognized publicly, to peers, superiors, and upper management. Such recognition increases both self-esteem and motivation.
- *Enhance the self-esteem and build the confidence of organization members.* Creative individuals are at their best when their minds are challenged—not their security or ego. Job security, adequate wages, and job satisfaction enhance an individual's self-confidence and security.
- *Improve communication so that ideas can be better shared.* This is certainly true within an organization. Creative individuals also have the need to com-municate with peers outside the organization; such activities should be en-couraged. Creative people needs a sounding board for their ideas and con-tinuous feedback from their efforts.
- *Place highly creative people in special jobs and provide training to take advantage of their creativity.* Establish career paths and financial rewards so as not to disadvantage creative people who are not part of the line organization. Maintain an entrepreneurial organization.

While creative climate is generally discussed within an organizational setting, research has recently shown that exercise—in particular, running—provides a unique personal climate for creative behavior.[26] Research surround-ing running and creativity reveals a consistent, positive relationship. A study at the Oregon Health Sciences Center showed that 54 percent of a group of more than 200 runners reported feeling in a trance or altered state of con-sciousness while running. Nearly 60 percent said that they became more creative while running. They felt that running helped them generate unique, spontaneous ideas with very little effort. Many of the subjects kept a pencil and paper in their lockers to write down their ideas after a workout. In another study, college students in two health classes ran three times a week, while students in a third class only listened to lectures. The runners showed big gains on a standard creativity test, while the nonrunners showed no improve-ment. Other studies showed similar results.

Both chemical and psychological reasons have been proposed to explain these results. Some feel that endorphins, released during exercise, promote altered states of consciousness that release creative energies. From a psycho-logical perspective, running allows the mind to free itself from stress and thus better tap into the unconscious. It has been suggested that headaches often occur because we focus on the past or future, which we cannot do anything about, rather than the present. Exercise helps us to focus better on the present and often relieves headaches. Organizations that provide exercise facilities and allow work time to be used for such activity may well be improving the creative potential of their employees.

APPLYING CREATIVE THINKING TECHNIQUES TO DESIGNING HEURISTIC ALGORITHMS[27]

Heuristics have become an important area of research and application in DS/MS. "Heuristic" is derived from a Greek word *heuriskein*, meaning "to discover." In this sense, a heuristic aims at studying the methods and rules of discovery or assisting in problem solving by systematically searching for good, but not necessarily optimal, solutions. Heuristics are simple procedures, often guided by common sense and creativity, for solving difficult problems. We can provide a rudimentary checklist for heuristic algorithm design. Heuristics should—

1. be simple, to facilitate user understanding and acceptance
2. have low computer storage requirements
3. be fast in terms of computational time
4. be accurate, having small average and mean square errors from optimality
5. be robust; that is, they should obtain good solutions for a wide variety of problems and not be too sensitive to changes in parameters
6. be capable of accepting multiple starting points, whether feasible or infeasible
7. produce multiple solutions (ideally in a single run), thus allowing the user to select the result that is most "satisficing"
8. have good stopping criteria that take advantage of search "learning" and avoid stagnation
9. provide interactive ability with the decision maker

A classification scheme for heuristics provides a means of idea generation for designing heuristic algorithms. Most heuristics fall into one or more of the following categories:

1. *Construction*. Construction algorithms generally start with an infeasible solution and progress toward a feasible solution by either adding or subtracting individual components one at a time until a feasible solution is obtained. "Greedy" algorithms fall into this category. For

instance, to find a solution to an integer knapsack problem

$$\max c_1 x_1 + \ldots + c_n x_n$$
$$a_1 x_1 + \ldots + a_n x_n \leqslant b$$
$$x_j = 0,1$$

one selects variables to be set equal to 1 in the order of nonincreasing c_j/a_j until no more can be added without violating the constraint. The minimum cost rule for finding an initial solution to a transportation problem is another example.

2. *Improvement*. Improvement algorithms begin with a feasible solution and successively improve it by exchanging or merging variables in a local search process. The simplex algorithm is an optimal improvement algorithm. The branch exchange heuristic for the traveling salesman problem is one example of an improvement heuristic. One simply removes two or three links from a traveling salesman tour and replaces them with others if the solution can be improved.

3. *Mathematical Programming*. Mathematical programming approaches use a mathematical optimization model and an exact solution procedure; then they modify this solution procedure to obtain a simpler and more efficient heuristic for the original problem. For instance, to solve an integer program, one might solve the linear program first and then find a nearby interior point that can be rounded to integer values without violating the binding constraints.

4. *Decomposition*. Decomposition refers to solving a sequence of smaller problems, the output of one being the input to the next, and then merging these solutions. For example, in a mixed-integer programming problem, one might obtain and keep a heuristic solution for the integer variables and then solve the remaining linear programming problem optimally for these fixed integer variables.

5. *Partitioning*. Partitioning algorithms break a problem into smaller subproblems, each of which is solved independently. These partial solutions are finally merged into a solution for the original problem. Breaking a routing problem down into geographical regions, each of which is solved separately, and then merging the routes into one would be an example.

6. *Restricting the Solution Space*. The idea here is to restrict the set of solutions so that a hard problem becomes easier to solve. For example, in a facilities layout problem, one might search only over solutions in which department shapes are rectangular. Or, one might change a nonlinear objective function into a linear objective function for simplicity.

7. *Relaxation*. This refers to expanding the solution space to simplify a problem. Lagrangian relaxation is a prime example.

In reviewing this classification, you can see many elements of creative thinking that we have discussed. For example, using Osborn's checklist, improvement heuristics use the principle of modifying a solution; mathematical programming uses adapting an existing solution technique; decomposition, partitioning, and solution space restriction use minifying; and relaxation uses magnifying.

What about the other element in Osborn's checklist? Could a heuristic that works well for one problem be used for a different one? What about combining them? Many heuristics first construct a solution and then improve it. Why not examine other combinations? What about rearranging steps in a heuristic? (We gave the example earlier of "route first and cluster second, or cluster first and route second" for vehicle routing problems.) Forced relationships might be used to develop new heuristics. For example, how might I combine improvement with decomposition? Designing heuristic procedures in DS/MS is a highly practical art in which the various techniques of creative thinking can be applied. Go back to originality exercise number 2. Can you now develop any different approaches to the traveling salesman problem? The design of effective heuristics in DS/MS represents one of the most creative challenges that both researchers and practitioners face, and provides one of the best opportunities for applying creativity enhancement techniques.

COMPUTER-BASED SUPPORT
FOR ENHANCING CREATIVITY

Lawrence Young has examined the role that computers might play in enhancing creativity.[28] Young defines **idea processing** as a process that takes ideas as inputs and produces as outputs the contextual frameworks we identify as decision problems or as plans. The importance of idea processing is summarized as follows:[29]

1. Extensive idea processing is directed at the recognition of significant decision problems or opportunities requiring decision making and action.
2. Extensive idea processing is necessary in defining and continuously redefining the scope and components of complex decision problems; that is, identifying the objectives and the factors that may affect achieving objectives.
3. Extensive idea processing is necessary to identify alternative strategies or action plans in complex decision-problem situations.
4. Idea processing, rather than following predefined rules or logical mathematical algorithms, is often the means by which a decision is made among alternative strategies.

The field of artificial intelligence, while concerned with capturing and processing human expertise, is fundamentally different from idea processing. Young argues that an expert system that could act as a creative consultant would have to be able to generate novel problem definitions, for instance, and offer them to human users for their judgment or reaction. It would then have to react to these human reactions with further explanations or improving modifications. The creation of a knowledge base that captures the complexities of creative human processes is rather unlikely at the present time.

Young advocates an engineering approach, that is, to derive designs from theory as well as possible. He proposes three generic levels of idea processing support:

Level 1: The "Secretarial" Level. The computer can be used essentially as a vehicle for capturing, recording, and mirroring back an individual's thoughts to facilitate further development.

Level 2: The "Framework-Paradigm" Level. The computer provides the user with selected frameworks that may be appropriate to the organization of the user's thoughts. These frameworks serve as thought-organizing aids, in a manner like checklists.

Level 3: The "Generative" Level. The computer is used to generate and display word-ideas for the user's consideration, by synthesizing or associating word elements.

Young suggests that the following idea-processing functions can be supported by computers:

1. Divergent search for alternative ideas, focusing on classification of ideas and arrangement of combinations
2. Problem redefinition and generalization, in which ideas are classified and arranged into logical hierarchies reflecting relative degrees of generality and specificity.
3. Idea manipulation aids, such as checklists
4. Metaphorical association, as in the context of synectics
5. Scenario building and analysis, in which key events or situational elements are summarized, stored, retrieved, and communicated in a historical sequence

Examples of each of these functions are provided for each of the levels listed above. We strongly suggest that interested readers consult Young's book for further elaboration. This subject is integrated into the general context of decision support systems.

Several computer programs, both commercial and experimental, have been developed to support creativity and idea processing.[30] The first commercial product was *ThinkTank* (Living Videotext, Mountain View, CA). ThinkTank, which spawned numerous competing products, is an outline processor that helps the user in thinking through hierarchically related concepts. Such programs relieve the user from many manual tasks so that more efficient cognitive effort can be expended, and they provide a dynamic visual "scratchpad" for working memory.

Consultant, a product of ODS, Inc., Palatine, IL, is a Macintosh-based program focused on using "your whole brain to think and work more productively." Among the product's features are a set of idea generation aids: Brainstormer, Questioner, Combiner, and Scenario. Brainstormer solicits a large number of user idea responses to a previously supplied stimulus question. Questioner uses a user-supplied question stem (for example, how can I write this chapter . . .?) in combination with a list of qualifiers or attributes (for example, better, more concisely, and so on) to generate questions. Combiner acts as a forced-relationship generator. Scenario leads the user through defining sequential events of a scenario.

Idea Generator Plus, published by Experience in Software, Berkeley, CA, develops problem-solving ideas by working with seven question-and-answer techniques to discover new points of view and solutions. The ideas, benefits, costs, and effects are evaluated.

Proctor describes experiments involving two computer-assisted creative problem-solving aids.[31] A program called *BRAIN* consists of three stages. In the first stage, problem definition, the user is encouraged to try to define or redefine a problem. In the second stage, idea generation, the computer scans the definition of the problem and replies with a semi-meaningful phrase. The user is then prompted to select from a list of randomly generated words or to enter an idea that may have occurred to him or her. The computer assists the user in generating more ideas. The last stage, synthesis, is focused on developing more "fully fledged" insights into the problem from the lists developed.

A second program discussed by Proctor, called *ORACLE*, acts as a process consultant that works with clients and helps them to define their own problems and identify their own solutions. *ORACLE* consists of a conversational interaction and a review section similar to *BRAIN*, which enables synthesis of ideas to take place. *ORACLE* challenges many of the perceptual blocks to creativity that we discussed in the previous chapter, such as assumptions, self-imposed barriers, one-correct-answer, fear of feeling foolish, and so on.

In an experiment with more than 170 subjects, Proctor found that over 50 percent generated what they considered to be at least one implementable new insight that they had not previously considered by using the programs. However, a significant proportion of subjects were less than enthusiastic about the value of the programs.

Elam and Mead have explored the issue of whether appropriately designed software can help individuals to be more creative in a controlled research experiment.[32] They developed a set of guidelines for designing creativity-enhancing decision support systems. In a laboratory experiment, they tested the following hypotheses:

Hypothesis 1. A user of a creativity-enhancing DSS will adopt a multiple-step decision process, whereas a user of no software will adopt a single-step decision process.

Hypothesis 2. The use of a creativity-enhancing DSS will result in higher levels of creative responses than the use of no software.

The experiment confirmed hypothesis 1. Elam and Mead found that differences in software versions influenced the level of creative responses. Thus, hypothesis 2 could not be confirmed. Their findings, however, support their proposition that a DSS designed to include qualitative as well as quantitative tools can contribute to higher levels of creativity.

Clearly, there is considerable potential for using computer support to enhance creativity. Considerable research remains to be done, and this appears to be a fruitful avenue for the future.

EXERCISES

1. In your factory, which produces glassware, products are packed in boxes using old newpapers to protect against breakage. The workers often waste time reading these newspapers. What ideas might you have to eliminate this problem?[33]

2. Ideas in business are often immediately rejected as being too costly. How can one be more creative in using this judgmental reasoning to develop better ideas?

3. Develop 25 list-making exercises to help one in deferring judgment and producing a greater quantity of ideas.

4. Develop new problem-sensitivity exercises like the ones in this chapter that are
    a. generic
    b. related to DS/MS

5. Develop new fluency exercises like the ones in this chapter that are
    a. generic
    b. related to DS/MS

6. Develop new flexibility exercises like the ones in this chapter that are
    a. generic
    b. related to DS/MS

7. Develop new originality exercises like . . . I think you get the picture by now!

8. Take something with which you are familiar and describe it in a strange fashion.

9. In making the strange familiar, how would you explain a complex algorithm like the simplex method to a layperson?

10. Apply Osborn's checklist to some important problem that you face.

11. Generate a list of synonyms for Osborn's key words, using a thesaurus. Do the new words suggest new ideas?

12. What ideas can you generate by using forced relationships for *each pair* of the following words: professor, student, fraternity, cafeteria, library?

13. Provide examples of how Osborn's checklist has been realized in everyday products. For example, minify: Walkman; combine: add mini-speakers to a Walkman; and so on.

14. List the attributes for
    a. pencil
    b. book
    c. simplex method
    d. a personal computer
    e. transportation model
    f. industrial robot
    g. MRP system

15. Using the attribute list from exercise 14, create a morphology for each thing or concept.

16. List ways in which organizations might achieve the recommendations for fostering creativity as discussed in the text.

17. Think of as many excuses as you can for breaking a date. (Watch your assumptions!)

18. Think of two of your fellow colleagues or students. List their individual strengths. Combine their strengths into a "superperson." What might this mean for teamwork and group problem solving?

19. A convenience store manager is disturbed by all the people who read magazines and wear them out without buying them. How might the manager solve this problem?

ENDNOTES

1. Min Basadur, George B. Graen, and Terri A. Scandura, "Training Effects on Attitudes Toward Divergent Thinking Among Manufacturing Engineers," *Journal of Applied Psychology* 71, no. 4 (1986): pp. 612–617.

2. Cited in J. Hadamard, *The Psychology of Invention in the Mathematical Field* (Princeton, NJ: Princeton University Press, 1945). Poincaré was one of the first to explore the role of the unconscious mind in the process of discovery. Hadamard draws and expands upon Poincaré's observations.

3. See, for example, Arthur B. VanGundy, *Creative Problem Solving: A Guide for*

Trainers and Management (New York: Quorum Books, 1987), and Sidney J. Parnes, R.B. Noller, and A.M. Biondi, eds., *Guide to Creative Action* (New York: Charles Scribner's Sons, 1977).

4. To solve this problem, you needed to test some basic assumptions. What assumptions did you make about each word, such as "cut" and "pieces"? Did you add any artificial constraints to the problem?

5. You look at your dashboard many times each time you drive, right? Are you aware of all the details? Probably not. We often assume that we know more about something than we actually do. This habit can easily carry over into problem solving. Testing assumptions is the only way to break this habit.

6. Like the dashboard exercise, this is not as easy as it seems. The use of "simple" models can become extremely routine, and we often lose sight of the basic assumptions of the models. In applying them, it is easy to overlook assumptions that are not true, thus *mis*applying the model. *Interfaces* often publishes "Misapplication Reviews." It is well worth the effort to study these examples.

7. This exercise is similar to the one asking for as many uses for a pencil as possible. If you try a new exercise like this each day, you will be amazed at how fluent you will become. (First try writing down as many exercises like this as you can!)

8. You probably would not have much trouble listing words that begin with each letter. This exercise is not much different. What might block your efforts is trying to make the sentences too logical. Thus, this exercise is designed to help overcome internal expressive blocks.

9. This exercise is somewhat different from the pure fluency exercises. You must first make a comparison and search for similarities or differences. However, you should not prejudge any ideas or force your thinking into too much of an analytical mode (for example, both can be drawn on a piece of paper).

10. Gene Woolsey, "The Fifth Column: The Dispatch Model That Was Too Simple, or What the Feds Don't Know Can't Hurt 'Em," *Interfaces* 13, no. 1 (February, 1983): pp. 76–78.

11. See A. Upton, R.W. Samson, and A.D. Farmer, *Creative Analysis* (New York: E.P. Dutton, 1978).

12. You might see a square made up of four triangles, or the top of a house, or an inverted roof, or two triangles consisting of two smaller ones, and so on. In this exercise you are required to switch visual perspectives and see the figure in different ways.

13. As noted in Chapter 2, we often get trapped into viewing DS/MS problems from only one perspective. Some of the most valuable insights can be found, however, from looking at problems differently. Hint to the graduate student: Try penalty functions.

14. Your first thought is probably linear programming. However, this problem can be just as easily modeled as a dynamic program and a network flow problem. How about simulation? What are the advantages or disadvantages of each approach?

15. This is probably more fun than English 101. In addition to developing originality, this exercise tests your ability to organize many pieces of information in a meaningful fashion. This ability is fundamental to problem formulation and modeling in DS/MS.

16. This is the famous "traveling salesman problem." Although it has been well-documented in the research literature, most undergraduate or beginning master's students have probably not seen it. The problem is simple enough so that many different rules of thumb, or heuristics, can be designed. The goal of this exercise is not to devise an optimal solution, but to develop heuristics that are original to the student. The design of heuristics provides a wonderful means of developing originality, and any "hard" combinatorial problem can be used. The last section of this chapter addresses this issue.

17. Niles Howard, "Business Probe: The Creative Spark," in *Creativity: The Art and Science of Business Management*, ed. A. Dale Timpe (New York: KEND Publishing, 1987), p. 6.

18. Gene Woolsey, "On Doing Operations Research in the Cracks or If the Error Isn't Within, It Must Be Between," *Interfaces* 6, no. 2 (February, 1976): pp. 42–44.

19. Cornelius H. Sullivan, Jr. and Charles E. Yates, "Reasoning by Analogy—A Tool for Business Planning," *Sloan Management Review* 29 (Spring 1988): pp. 55–60.

20. G.A. Davis and J. A. Scott, eds., *Training Creative Thinking* (Huntington, NY: Krieger, 1978).

21. See Leonard W. Swanson, *Linear Programming, Basic Theory and Applications* (New York: McGraw-Hill, 1980), and Jeffrey Camm et al. "The Calhoun Textile Mill Case: An Exercise on the Significance of Linear Programming Model Formulation," *IIE Transactions* 19, no. 1: pp. 23–28.

22. George Polya, *How To Solve It*, 2d ed. (Garden City, NY: Doubleday, Anchor Books, 1957); *Mathematical Discovery*, vol. I (New York: John Wiley & Sons, 1962); and *Mathematical Discovery*, vol. II (New York: John Wiley & Sons, 1965). These books are perhaps the best sources for creative problem-solving in mathematics. These books have numerous examples from algebra, geometry, and elementary combinatorics along with a variety of problem-solving hints from the author's experience. Volume II, particularly a chapter entitled, "On Learning, Teaching, and Learning Teaching," is well worth reading for any instructors of quantitative disciplines.

23. See James R. Evans and Jeffrey D. Camm, "Using Pictorial Representations in Teaching Linear Programming Modeling," *IIE Transactions* 22 (1990): pp. 191–95.

24. For other examples of morphological analysis applied to operations research, see Heiner Muller-Merbach, "The Use of Morphological Techniques for OR-Approaches to Problems," *Operational Research '75, Proceedings of the Seventh IFORS International Conference on Operational Research*, Tokyo, Japan, July 17–23, 1975, ed K.B. Haley (Amsterdam: North-Holland Publishing, 1976).

25.   Mark R. Edwards and J. Ruth Sproull, "Creativity: Productivity Gold Mine?" *Journal of Creative Behavior* 18, no. 3 (1984): pp. 175–84, and Michael K. Badawy, "How to Prevent Creativity Mismanagement," *Research Management* 29, no. 4 (1986): p. 28.

26.   J. Scott Hinkle and Bruce W. Tuckman, "Chasing the Muse," *Runner's World*, November 1988, pp. 77–82.

27.   For discussions of both practical implications and research issues involving heuristics, see S.H. Zanakis and J.R. Evans, "Heuristic 'Optimization': Why, When, and How to Use It," *Interfaces* 11, no. 5 (October 1981): pp. 84–91, and S.H. Zanakis, J.R. Evans, and A.A. Vazacopoulos, "Heuristic Methods and Applications: A Categorized Survey," *European Journal of Operational Research* 43 (1989): pp. 88–110. See also H. Muller-Merbach, "A Five Facets Frame for the Design of Heuristics," *European Journal of Operational Research* 17 (1984): pp. 313–16. This paper suggests the need for creative thinking techniques to heuristic design. This section is adapted from these articles and is probably more relevant to graduate students than to undergraduate students.

28.   Lawrence F. Young, *Decision Support and Idea Processing Systems* (Dubuque, IA: Wm. C. Brown Publishers, 1989).

29.   *Ibid.*, p. 247.

30.   Chapter 10 of Young's book describes *ThinkTank* and *Consultant* in considerable detail, with numerous examples of their use.

31.   T. Proctor, "Experiments With Two Computer Assisted Creative Problem Solving Aids," *Omega, The International Journal of Management Science* 17, no. 2 (1989): pp. 197–200.

32.   Joyce J. Elam and Melissa Mead, "Can Software Influence Creativity?" *Information Systems Research* 1, no. 1 (1990): pp. 1–22.

33.   This exercise is adapted from Parnes et al., eds., *Guide to Creative Action*, p. 333.

CHAPTER 5
Creativity and Problem-Solving Methodologies

INTRODUCTION

In the last two chapters, we discussed the general nature of creative thinking and presented techniques for stimulating ideas and enhancing one's creativity. In this chapter we focus on the role of creative thinking in problem solving, particularly its implications in the decision and management sciences. We shall introduce the **Osborn-Parnes Creative Problem-Solving Process**—a structured methodology for problem solving that provides a practical approach to addressing problems found in any discipline.

EVOLUTION OF THE CREATIVE PROBLEM-SOLVING PROCESS[1]

In Chapter 3 we introduced Wallas's descriptive model of problem solving. He described problem solving as a four-step process:

1. preparation
2. incubation
3. inspiration
4. verification

While this model of problem solving is often used to *explain* how ideas are born, it does not provide any systematic guidelines for producing ideas.

After all, how can we consciously become inspired? This model simply describes how creative ideas result from unconscious thought. Clearly, such a descriptive model is not useful for *enhancing* problem-solving abilities. A normative approach is required.

A variety of normative problem-solving processes have been proposed by workers in various fields of study. Each of these processes requires analytical, judicial, and creative thinking, but with different emphases. One of the earliest normative problem-solving processes was proposed by Dewey.[2] He characterized the problem-solving process in three phases:

1. defining the problem
2. identifying the alternatives
3. selecting the best alternative

Simon's three-stage process of intelligence, design, and choice, briefly discussed in Chapter 2, is similar. In the intelligence stage, the problem is recognized and information is gathered for defining the problem. In the design stage, solutions are developed. In the choice stage, the solution alternatives are selected and implemented. Most other problem-solving models are variants of this three-step process. A partial list is given in Table 5-1. A paper by McPherson provides a more complete description.[3]

Alex Osborn is credited with laying the foundation for the modern creative problem-solving process. Osborn, who developed brainstorming, described the creative-thinking process in three stages:

1. fact-finding
2. idea-finding
3. solution-finding

Osborn's work influenced psychologist Sidney J. Parnes. Parnes made three major improvements to Osborn's model.[4] He recognized the importance of solving the right problem before forging ahead to develop ideas. Thus, he added a **problem-finding stage** between the fact-finding and idea-finding stages. He also recognized the importance of implementation and added an **acceptance-finding stage** after solution-finding. Finally, he recognized that problem solving begins with an awareness about some ambiguous challenge, concern, or opportunity; in short, a "mess." Therefore, the process begins with a **mess-finding stage**. The complete process, which we shall refer to as the Osborn-Parnes Creative Problem-Solving (CPS) Process, is

1. mess-finding
2. fact-finding
3. problem-finding
4. idea-finding
5. solution-finding
6. acceptance-finding

Table 5-1 Some Structured Problem-Solving Processes (Adapted from McPherson)

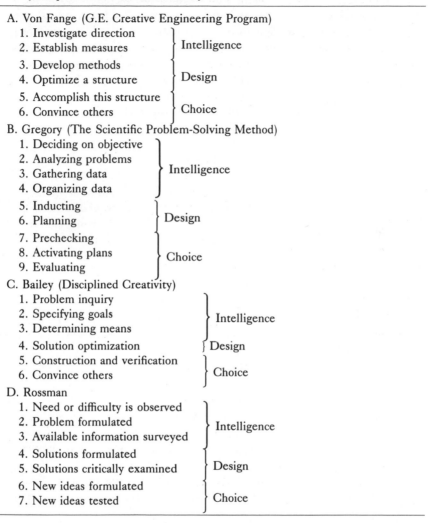

A. Von Fange (G.E. Creative Engineering Program)
  1. Investigate direction ⎱
  2. Establish measures   ⎰ Intelligence
  3. Develop methods ⎱
  4. Optimize a structure ⎰ Design
  5. Accomplish this structure ⎱
  6. Convince others ⎰ Choice

B. Gregory (The Scientific Problem-Solving Method)
  1. Deciding on objective ⎱
  2. Analyzing problems
  3. Gathering data ⎰ Intelligence
  4. Organizing data
  5. Inducting ⎱
  6. Planning ⎰ Design
  7. Prechecking ⎱
  8. Activating plans ⎰ Choice
  9. Evaluating

C. Bailey (Disciplined Creativity)
  1. Problem inquiry ⎱
  2. Specifying goals ⎰ Intelligence
  3. Determining means
  4. Solution optimization ⎰ Design
  5. Construction and verification ⎱
  6. Convince others ⎰ Choice

D. Rossman
  1. Need or difficulty is observed ⎱
  2. Problem formulated ⎰ Intelligence
  3. Available information surveyed
  4. Solutions formulated ⎱
  5. Solutions critically examined ⎰ Design
  6. New ideas formulated ⎱
  7. New ideas tested ⎰ Choice

Recall that we stated that a problem exists if there is a gap between some current and some desired states of affairs. In most cases there are many problems, often intertwined; that is, a **mess**. Recognizing the existence of a mess is a necessary first step in problem solving. Thus, **mess-finding** involves becoming aware of challenges and opportunities. Often only a vague perception of a deviation between current and desired states of affairs exists. The purpose of this stage is to clarify the goals on which to focus problem-solving effort. **Fact-finding** is an information-gathering task designed to increase our understanding of the mess. From an analysis of this information, initial problem definitions may materialize. The **problem-finding** phase is focused on developing and refining problem statements that will address the mess. A well-known adage is that "A problem well-defined is half-solved," yet we often pay very little attention to this step. **Idea-finding** is devoted to generating as many potential ideas or solutions as possible. Specific techniques such as checklists, brainstorming, forced relationships, or morphological analysis, which we discussed in Chapter 3, can be used effectively for idea generation. In the **solution-finding** stage, potential solutions are evaluated, judged, and selected. Finally, **acceptance-finding** is focused on overcoming barriers to implementation.

This process, when consciously applied, explicitly resolves each of the major difficulties to problem solving that we discussed before: failure to recognize the existence of a problem, failure to use all available information, failure to define the correct problem, failure to recognize or question assumptions, failure to consider and evaluate a wide range of alternatives, and failure to address implementation issues. Furthermore, it is not necessary to follow this process sequentially. In many situations, for instance, the problem is clearly defined (hopefully correctly!), and one might begin with the idea-finding stage. In other situations, the mess needs to be delineated more clearly. Remember that one of the important characteristics of a creative problem solver is **flexibility**; this applies to the use of the CPS process also.

Fundamental to applying CPS are the notions of **divergence** and **convergence**. Divergent thinking focuses on the generation of alternative ideas or approaches; convergent thinking focuses on a choice. Each stage of CPS involves both divergent and convergent thought. For example, in fact-finding, one begins by gathering a wide variety of possible facts, whether or not they are relevant (that is, deferring judgment and striving for quantity). This is the divergent phase. After the facts have been collected, we separate the relevant from irrelevant (the convergent phase). Similar activities occur in each of the other stages of the process. You can now see why fluency and flexibility are important traits for the creative problem solver.

In the remainder of this chapter we shall discuss in more detail the individual stages of the Osborn-Parnes creative problem-solving process, with a particular focus on their use and implications in DS/MS.

MESS-FINDING

An important job of a manager is to solve problems. However, to do this, he or she must first *identify* the problems. Mess-finding is concerned with sensing an awareness of the challenges, concerns, and opportunities within the system and selecting the important objectives. Russell Ackoff defines a **mess** as a system of external conditions that produces dissatisfaction; alternatively, a mess can be conceptualized as a system of problems.[5] The interaction among the problems generally is complicated and not clearly understood.[6] Taken as a system, problems do not exist in isolation; each affects the fate of the mess of which they are a part. The "solution" to a mess is therefore not a simple sum of the solutions to problems that can be extracted from it.

Woolsey provides a good example of a mess:

The Foundry Problem

Some time ago in a far city there was a manufacturing firm that was in a most happy state. Demand for their product far outstripped the ability to supply it. Their quality was so high that customers did accept the long lead times, rather than go to a vendor of less excellence. The profit margin on the products was comfortable, and soon the company found itself forced, happily, to go to a three-shift operation. However, it was not long before it was noticed that the part of the firm that did the final assembly and finishing was posting service rates to customers that were poor indeed. In fact, only with the greatest effort could the service rate of on-time deliveries reach 37%. What made this doubly strange was that the part of the firm that did the initial foundry work on the product was posting rates of 99.995% of desired tonnage. There was little question in the minds of management that the finishing and assembly shop needed looking into.[7]

We can usually divide messes in business and industry into two classes: those involving systems design and those involving systems improvement.[8] A systems-design mess is one in which an organization must face an issue that has not arisen before and therefore has no precedent. A systems-improvement mess is one in which the organization voluntarily entertains disturbances and seeks to do things differently.

Mess-finding is also related to the level of management of the decision maker. Individuals in lower levels of an organization are primarily concerned with the technology they manage and are not sensitive to broader messes within the organization. As one moves up the managerial hierarchy, perspectives on messes will change. Messes will become messier as one deals more with organizational and environmental concerns. This aspect can be particularly troublesome to management scientists who are accustomed to working with clearly defined problems of technology in operational contexts. Such activities often are not recognized by higher levels of management, who require justification for the consultants' employment. A high level of problem sensitivity and awareness of managerial messes is therefore a top priority for the DS/MS consultant. The advice suggested to the engineer/mathematician is to get an MBA and learn about the business environment.

All managers maintain lists of messes or problems that require study and action. Mess-finding often is the result of observing an unexpected occurrence or a signal of a potential problem, such as low profits, poor quality, loss of market share, or employee absenteeism—or observation of some pattern in a series of events.[9] For example, in the foundry problem, we see an awareness of poor customer service along with the seemingly paradoxical fact that the foundry was working at a high level of productivity. However, this mode of mess recognition is **reactive**. Managers and decision scientists need to be **proactive** and *seek* messes. This is one of the principal messages of the quality gurus: never stop looking for ways to improve the system continually. However, it is generally quite difficult to define the process by which messes are discovered.

Using an empirical study of managers, Pounds studied the process of mess recognition.[10] He interviewed, observed, and questioned about 50 executives in a large, technically based corporation. The executives were asked to describe the problems they faced and the processes by which they had become aware of these problems. Observations were made of meetings during which problems were identified, discussed, and sometimes solved. Investigations were made of the sources and disposition of several specific problems. Finally, a questionnaire was developed and administered to each executive who participated in the study.

Pounds based his study on the assumption that problems are characterized as differences between some existing situation and some desired situation. For example, if a manager states that a quality problem exists, then the manager must have some baseline measure of good quality relative to the existing level of quality. Hence, the process of mess-finding is based on defining these differences. Pounds suggests that managers define differences by comparing what they perceive to be the output of some "model" (not necessarily a mathematical model!) that predicts the values of the same variables. In the case of a quality problem, this might be a comparison of actual quality costs as a percentage of sales to expert recommendations of 2.5 percent. The cost model is the model used to define the difference. In the foundry problem, the model probably involved the comparison of a 37 percent service rate to an ideal rate that was expected to be much higher.

Several standards for comparison exist. First, one might compare performance with *some other reference group* (1st and 2nd shifts). Second, one can compare to a *universal standard* (4.0 GPA, .300 batting average, par golf). Third, a comparison may be made with *prior performance* (what the company did in the same quarter last year). Finally, one may use a *synethetic standard*—an arbitrary target (desired market share).

Thus, Pounds proposed a four-stage model of the process. The first stage consists of choosing a conceptual model as a basis and making outcome predictions from it. The second stage is to compare the predictions to reality. In the remaining two stages, the differences are identified, and one or more of them is selected for problem solving. According to Pounds, the problem of mess-finding is therefore reduced to the problem of understanding the models that managers use to define differences.

Cowan proposed a theoretical model of mess recognition.[11] The process consists of three general stages: gestation/latency, categorization, and diagnosis. The gestation/latency stage represents the period before any problem-recognition activity. Gestation refers to situations where conditions in the environment are changing and building toward recognition. For example, an employee might become more and more frustrated with work, but the supervisor may not be aware of the trouble. Some triggering event may force recognition of a problem, or the individual may become more sensitive to the situation over time (latency). Categorization refers to the process by which an individual notices that a problem exists but cannot fully describe the problem. Diagnosis is required to describe adequately the perceived problematic situation. This involves searching for additional information to achieve greater certainty about a problem description.

Smith provides a more comprehensive study of mess identification.[12] Smith suggests several means of explaining mess identification. One means is the cognitive process as exemplified by the "Aha!" experience. For example, in the movie *The China Syndrome*, the operations manager of a nuclear power plant identified major structural flaws in the plant from having noticed the rippling of his coffee after an earth tremor. A second means is the individual's role-related activity. For instance, if an individual's function is to review operating reports, such a review function would often identify messes, since the individual would be comparing the reports to some model in his or her mind. Organizations routinely collect and monitor data on certain indicators. Mess identification can often be explained in terms of organizational roles and procedures. The third means of mess identification is personal motivation. For example, the need to keep one's job, monetary rewards, recognition, and so on can be motivating factors to seek and improve messes. By identifying appropriate problems, one can propose solutions and promote acceptance of an action desired for reasons unrelated to the problems' existence. The story by Simkin and Daniels on the $10 million hospital parking garage in Chapter 3 is one example; the garage was one manager's pet project, and it was *his* conclusion that a parking problem existed. The final means of mess identification suggested by Smith is the nature and manifestation of the problem itself. A single event, such as an angry call from a customer, might cause a mess to be identified.

Perceptions and frames of reference can influence mess recognition.[13] Problems are not objective things; they vary in the way different individuals conceptualize the situation. For example, the sound of an aircraft may be perceived as a problem to those on the ground but not to the passengers and flight crew. The degree of structure in a mess also influences one's ability to recognize and correctly identify it.

We can enhance mess-finding through creative-thinking principles. As a creative process, mess-finding involves both divergent and convergent activities. Divergent thinking involves generating goals and constraints in the system. VanGundy suggests two basic questions in the divergent stage: *Wouldn't It Be Nice If?* and *Wouldn't It Be Awful If?*[14] For instance, consider the foundry problem and assume that management was not aware of the poor delivery rate. Some questions that management might consider would be: Wouldn't it be nice if we could satisfy 100 percent of delivery promises? (This might uncover the poor delivery rate problem.) Wouldn't it be nice if we could produce all our customers' demand without requiring three shifts? (This might suggest a mess involving poor capacity planning or production scheduling). Wouldn't it be awful if customers stopped ordering our product? (In developing reasons why customers might stop ordering, the customer delivery rate might be suggested, again leading to an awareness of the problem.) This process is followed by convergent thinking that involves an assessment of the ownership of the mess, how familiar one is with it, how important it is, and how soon it must be resolved. Management might very well be alarmed at the poor service rate, identify the owner of the mess as the plant manager, and require immediate resolution.

Graham and Jahani propose that mess-finding requires high-level managers representing all facets of the organization and interacting in a group with the intent of defining problems.[15] They suggest that both the organization and its environment be considered as part of a larger system. The members of this system are called "stakeholders" and consist of those who either affect the products of the organization and its efficiency of production or are affected by the organization. Problems arise from the actions of the stakeholders. Graham and Jahani describe a systems approach in which one first identifies the stakeholders and their degree of importance to the organization. Second, one lists the actions that each stakeholder may take, ranking these also in order of importance. A quantitative measure of stakeholder-action pairs is computed, resulting in a priority ordering of management perceptions of sources of future problems. A major benefit of this approach is that it forces people to think in terms of stakeholders' future actions; as a group process, the problems identified will represent the perceptions of the group as a whole, rather than those of one or two of the most vocal or argumentative members.

A critical aspect of mess-finding is the choice of a measure of effectiveness (MOE) on which to base perceptions of problems.[16] We use measures of effectiveness to find out how well an existing system works and what it is worth. That is, MOEs predict or evaluate performance in the organization. In the foundry problem, for example, the percentage of on-time deliveries was the critical MOE in recognizing that a problem existed.

Measures of effectiveness should be operationally credible; that is, they should relate to some benefit, have some predictive value, and be sensitive to factors known to influence the value. They must also be measurable; that is, they should be determinable from available data. Uncertainties always exist in choosing MOEs, and poor choices can lead to incorrect identification of messes. U.S. firms have received much criticism lately for using short-term profits as the principal measure of effectiveness instead of long-term measures such as quality and competitive position.

How can an organization increase the chances of finding messes (or opportunities)? Some mechanisms include holding regular staff meetings, going to professional conferences, visiting competitors, and reading trade journals. Many times it is hearing about others' problems or solutions that leads to the identification of one's own messes.

FACT-FINDING

The purpose of fact-finding is to gather as much information as possible to increase understanding about the mess. The more information one has, the better one can consider different problem perspectives during the problem-finding stage and begin to generate potential solutions during the idea-finding stage. Creative ideas often result from careful observation of unusual occurrences.

Fact-finding helps to avoid premature evaluation of the specific problems entwined in the mess and allows one to focus on the mess rather than the solution. It may also help one uncover unanticipated or overlooked aspects of the mess. Additional data can sometimes provide new perspectives and understanding for problem resolution.

As with mess-finding, fact-finding is a two-stage process of divergent and convergent thinking. During divergence, one attempts to draw out relevant information about the mess using the questions who? what? when? where? why? and how? Urban suggests that studies be conducted to determine (1) existing models or rules of thumb, (2) the characteristics of the decision process (who decides, when, and on what basis?), (3) the existing flow and usage of information, (4) the clientele's behavior and relationship to the organization, (5) the stated and apparent goals of the organization, (6) the information and formal organization structure, (7) managers' definitions of their perceived problems, and (8) the basic issues underlying current crises.[17] These activities could be done by extensive interviews with managers, a study of recent and ongoing decisions, probing questionnaires, and considerations of managers' perceptions. As new information is uncovered and analyzed, new perspectives often emerge.

VanGundy suggests using general checklists of questions in addition to those noted above.[18] Some examples are:

1. What do you know about the situation?
2. What would be better if you resolved this situation? What would be worse?
3. What is the major obstacle facing you in dealing with this situation?
4. What parts of the situation are related?
5. When is the situation likely to get worse? Get better?

In the foundry problem, some of the facts uncovered about the mess were:[19]

1. In the finishing shop, many machines were idle for lack of work on any shift.
2. The product came in sets of 100 units.
3. The foundry produced castings for the finishing shop to work on, but the finishing shop often did not get enough good castings to make up a set.

4. The finishing shop had other priority jobs following the incomplete job; so the partial set was usually placed in a holding warehouse until they could get back to it to complete the set.
5. Upon examining the holding warehouse, a multitude of incomplete sets were discovered, and virtually no completed sets were found in the warehouse.
6. Setups of parts took five to ten hours of machine setup time but only a few minutes of running time.
7. Customers would not accept incomplete shipments.

Note that we simply listed a set of facts; no attempt was made at this point to determine their relevance.

Fact-finding deals with clarifying assumptions and constraints to bring manageability to a mess and lead to succinct problem definitions. We refer to this as "problem structuring." Four streams of problem structuring have been identified in practice.[20] These are checklists, formal modeling, systems analysis, and a "people" approach stressing intangible, interpersonal, and organizational factors.

The Kepner and Tregoe method is an example of a checklist approach.[21] A diagnosis of the mess is obtained by answering the following questions:

1. What is the deviation (versus what it is not)?
2. When did the deviation occur (versus when it did not occur)?
3. Where did the deviation occur (versus where it did not occur)?
4. To what extent did the deviation occur (versus to what extent it did not occur)?
5. Who is associated with the deviation (versus who is not associated with it)?

Notice that the key word *why* is missing. This is because it does not make sense to ask "why" at this stage of problem analysis, since one does not have enough information. The expectation of such an approach is that the answers to a checklist of questions will lead to a correctly structured problem. However, the use of checklists tend to restrict one into a convergent, rather than a divergent, train of thought.

Formal modeling approaches, such as operations research, revolve around a (mathematical) model. The difficulty with such approaches is that not all problems can or should be addressed in this fashion, and all information cannot be captured as variables and constraints.

The systems approach, involving the gathering of quantitative data, provides a more realistic approach in that it assumes that problem structuring is complex and should not be regarded as something to be completed quickly. This approach is closer to the fact-finding phase within the creative problem-solving framework.

The final approach suggests that problems are not concrete entities but rather phenomena defined by differences in perceptions by individuals and groups. The focus is away from things and towards people.

Simple data-collection methods such as check sheets (Figure 5-1) are useful in fact-finding. The literature often discusses the role of accounting data in problem solving.[22] Accounting data must be viewed carefully; Graham refutes these four commonly held beliefs about data:[23]

1. Data reflects a constant reality.
2. People are behaving according to the rules.
3. People will do what they say for the reasons they say.
4. Production of data is not affected by organizational politics.

One should also consider using all the senses: seeing, hearing, touching, smelling, and tasting. The senses are used extensively in the fine arts. Since our premise is that creative problem solving is also an art, it makes sense to consider them. Gene Woolsey provides many examples of using sensory perception in fact-finding. In one particularly amusing story, he observes that every time he walks into a warehouse with pallets two deep, he knows he is going to make some money. Simply

> ... look closely at boxes on the *second* pallet back at the *top* level. You are looking for dust. Every box found with discernible dust on the side should be

Figure 5-1 An Example of a Check Sheet for Recording Errors in Outpatient Insurance Billing in a Hospital

Patient ID Date Error Code	ERROR CODES
	01 — POLICY # MISSING
	02 — POLICY # INCORRECT
	03 — SOC. SEC. # MISSING
	04 — SOC. SEC. # INCORRECT
	05 — EMPLOYER NAME MISSING
	06 — EMPLOYER NAME INCORRECT
	07 — EMPLOYER ADDRESS MISSING
	08 — EMPLOYER ADDRESS INCORRECT
	09 — DATE OF INJURY MISSING
	10 — DATE OF INJURY INCORRECT
	11 — AUTO INSURANCE MISSING
	12 — AUTO INSURANCE INCORRECT
	13 — CHIEF COMPLAINT MISSING
	14 — CHIEF COMPLAINT INCORRECT
	15 — RETURN BY INS. CO.
	16 — ALL INS. INFO. MISSING
	17 — INSURANCE ADDRESS MISSING
	18 — INSURANCE ADDRESS INCORRECT
	19 — INSURANCE NAME MISSING
	20 — INSURANCE NAME INCORRECT
	21 —
	22 —
	23 —

recorded by the cost accountant. If the majority of boxes on the second pallet at the top level exhibit dust, then we proceed . . . [to] examine the second pallet at the second level . . . . If the majority of second pallets on the second level exhibit dust, we then proceed to . . . examine the second pallets on the first level. If *these* show dust on the sides, I start planning vacations in Bermuda.[24]

Some of Woolsey's standard fact-finding questions in dealing with inventory are, "How much is (this part) worth?" "How many of these are in the bin?" "How long has this bin been here?" and "What's your cost of money for this company?"

The convergent phase of fact-finding deals with extracting only the information that is most useful, so that the problem can be refined. During fact-finding, we try to separate relevant data from irrelevant data. One way to narrow down the collection of facts is first to highlight all the relevant or interesting ones. From this collection, try to identify groups of facts that have something in common. Which groups of facts are most critical to the mess? These should then be prioritized. From this list, you can probably write down a tentative problem definition and proceed to the problem-finding stage.

The problem-classification schemes that we discussed in Chapter 1 can be useful aids in fact-finding (but they should not be considered as methods for *problem*-finding). Classification schemes provide ideas about the types of data for which to search.

Many formal techniques to help in fact-finding can be found in the systems-analysis literature. Flowcharts are among the most elementary tools and are highly recommended in quality problem solving. A systems flowchart is simply a step-by-step description of how a process operates. An example is given in Figure 5-2. Flowcharts help one to understand a system better and to visualize the relationships and sequence among system elements. Other techniques for identifying the complex interactions among the many elements in systems are graphs and interaction matrices.[25]

Woolsey is an advocate of working within the system to gather facts on how the system *really* operates. One story of his involves a regional transportation district that had overbought its winter supply of antifreeze and was taking considerable heat from the local press.[26] A professor offered to come in with some students and do a study on the situation (as a public service). The civil servant proposed that "they have an immediate brainstorming session to come up with ideas to (1) get the press off of their case and (2) try to solve the mess somehow." (Notice the suggestion of immediately jumping from mess-finding to idea-finding!) The professor proposed an alternative, suggesting that he and his students take a few days and learn how the computer system worked for ordering and stocking inventory in the warehouse. This would include working a couple of weeks in the warehouse as inventory clerks, handing out parts, reordering, and restocking. Next, they would take some more time to learn the purchasing side of the inventory system and work a couple of weeks in purchasing, ordering parts. When the civil servant asked

**Figure 5-2 Partial System Flowchart of
Hospital Emergency Admissions Process**

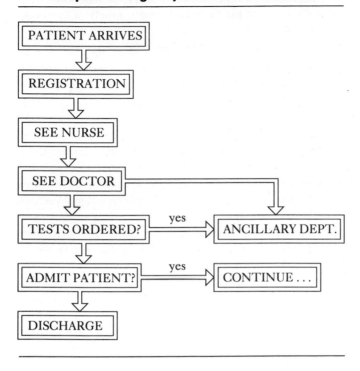

"Couldn't you learn as much by watching?" the professor pointed out that
"there were some things one could learn only by doing."

PROBLEM-FINDING

Mess-finding and fact-finding pave the way for problem-finding—the
development of a problem statement for the *real* problem, which can be used
to generate potential solutions. In DS/MS, one usually *assumes* that the problem has been identified and that the task of the analyst is to find a solution.
Managers, however, are more interested in the correct specification of their
decision problems. **Problem formulation** (the term most often used in DS/
MS) is the process of formulating the present set of conditions, symptoms,
causes, and triggering events into a problem or set of problems sufficiently
well specified so that the risk of using analytical procedures to solve the wrong
problem is minimized.[27] In creative problem solving, we use the term problem-
finding to describe this activity.

The way a problem is stated can have a significant effect on the solution.[28] Often, the correct definition of a problem may lead to a creative solution that would otherwise not have been discovered. Drucker noted:

> Indeed, the most common source of mistakes in management decisions is the emphasis on finding the right answer rather than the right question. . . . The important and difficult job is never to find the right answer, it is to find the right question. For there are few things as useless—if not as dangerous—as the right answer to the wrong question.[29]

However, little is known in general, either through theoretical or empirical study, about the nature of problem finding and its relation to problem solving.[30] We do know, however, that there is a very real tendency to deal with *symptoms* of problems rather than the problems themselves. For instance, the question of how to dam an overflowing river does not address the more basic problem of how to protect property from floods. Thus it is vitally important that we be able to find the true problems within a mess.

Review once again the foundry problem and the set of facts presented in the last section. What problems can you state? Use the space below to write down your ideas.

In this example, the foundry shop was producing right up to its tons-per-month goal. This was its measure of performance; in the foundry shop's view, the fact that the tonnage produced contained many incomplete sets was not its problem—it was the finishing shop's problem. The real problem in this mess was how to find a motivational method to get more complete sets to the finishing shop.[31]

The term "type III error" is often used to characterize solving the wrong problem.[32] Managers often ignore this type of error, and consequently much effort and expense are wasted on irrelevant problem solving. A major source of type III error is confusion between causes and symptoms, often due to a lack of adequate fact-finding. As an example, it has been reported that assumptions about the physics of corn popping have probably been flawed, leading popcorn scientists to seek the wrong solution to a problem.[33] Popcorn pops when the moisture inside a kernel is heated to 480 degrees and steam builds up the pressure inside the kernel to about 135 pounds per square inch. The kernel explodes in a puff of starch, and protein materializes in its place. Scientists had believed that if the outer sheath of a kernel were damaged, this would create leaks through which steam could escape without building up the necessary popping pressure. Experiments have found that this is not so critical an issue. The *real problem* is to improve the uniformity of moisture in the kernels so that all kernels in the batch explode at roughly the same time.

Another cause of type III error is defining a problem in terms of familiar solutions or methodologies, such as when an LP modeling approach is taken at the outset of a study. Significant type III errors often result when consultants are brought into the solution phase of a DS/MS study, rather than into the mess-finding phase. The author was involved in such a case.

I was asked to develop an optimization routine to "minimize the percentage of scrap" in a cutting-stock situation. The client had an effective computer routine for generating and evaluating cutting patterns, but he did not have the expertise to address the associated combinatorial optimization problem of selecting the best combination of patterns for a set of orders. Thus, the problem seemed a straightforward application of implicit enumeration. However, very little improvement over the existing method was found after implementing the algorithm, until I observed that different-sized stock was used to generate the cutting patterns. A *small percentage* of scrap on a large piece of stock generated a *large amount* of scrap. Redefinition of the problem to minimize the *amount* of scrap, rather than the percentage of scrap, resulted in significant savings.

In Chapter 3 we noted that individuals tend to solve problems using the tools that they have. The same holds true for problem-finding. If an engineer is told that there is a production problem in a plant and is asked to investigate it, he or she will seek and find an engineering problem and solution. Similarly, if the same problem is given to a behavioral scientist, he or she will seek and find a behavioral problem and solution. A management scientist trained in mathematical programming will seek and find a mathematical programming (resource allocation) problem and solution, and so on. The tendency to classify problems, which we discussed in Chapter 2, adds to such fixations. Past experience with similar problems *is* useful in finding analogies that often facilitate problem solving. However, this can easily lead to incorrect problem identification. Such functional fixation is one of the barriers to creativity that we seek to break. By recognizing the potential bias of background and training, we can avoid these influences.

A good problem statement for creative problem solving has four major elements: an "invitational stem," an ownership component, an action component, and a goal component.[34] The invitational stem is, "In what ways might . . .?" This encourages a divergent response, rather than using "How . . .?" A problem statement must also indicate who owns the problem; thus, an ownership component must be specified. An action verb in conjunction with the goal component is needed to specify what is to be done. Some examples of problem statements are:

> In what ways might I model this problem?
> In what ways might I solve the model?
> In what ways might this company improve productivity?
> In what ways might the production manager schedule the jobs?

In the first statement, ownership is specified by "I," the action verb is "model," and "this problem" is the goal component. VanGundy offers several suggestions for writing good problem statements:[35]

1. Avoid including problem criteria in your statements.
2. Generate as many statements as you can. (When managers diagnose a managerial problem they tend to develop only one world view or perspective.)[36]
3. Keep your statements as brief as possible; be concise.
4. Don't be afraid to list "silly" statements.
5. Always include ownership and action components.
6. Include only one problem area at a time in each statement.
7. If you are dissatisfied with your statements, use stimulator techniques (as discussed in Chapter 3) or recycle to mess-finding or fact-finding.

Problem-finding is a divergent-convergent activity in which alternate statements are generated and subsequently evaluated to capture the real problem. The divergent phase of problem-finding begins with a review of the data generated during fact-finding. Develop lists of possible ownership and action elements, striving for quantity. Next, consider different combinations from each list and examine the problem statements that are suggested. Techniques such as repeatedly asking "why" often prove useful for redefining a problem. The answer to "why" will often provide a new and more basic statement of the problem. For example, consider the statement "In what ways might I model this problem?"

> Ask why: "Why do I want to model this problem?"
> Answer: "To solve it using a computer."
> Redefine: "In what ways might I solve it on a computer?"
> Ask why: "Why do I want to solve it on a computer?"
> Answer: "To take advantage of the software that I have."

Redefine: "In what ways might I take advantage of the software that I have?"

and so on.

It is easy to see that new problem perspectives develop through this redefinition process. For example, the appropriate model might be obvious after one examines the software that is available.

A classic example of problem redefinition, the elevator problem, can be found in Volkema:[37]

> A manager of a large office building has been receiving an increasing number of complaints about the building's elevator service, particularly during rush hours. Several of the larger tenants in the building have threatened to move out unless the service is improved. In response, the building manager recently inquired into the possibility of adding one or two elevators to the building. Although it would be feasible, the only elevator company in the area has a six-month backlog of orders. As an assistant to the manager, you were asked to come up with a plan to get two new elevators installed within three months. You must present the plan at the next staff meeting.

The problem that has been posed is, "In what ways can I get two new elevators installed within three months?" Using the "why" method, we might redefine the problem as, "In what ways can I improve the elevator service?" Again asking "why," we might obtain a further redefinition: "In what ways might I reduce the number of complaints from tenants?" Which of these is the real problem? Can you think of a creative solution?[38]

Analogy represents another technique for redefining problems. (Recall that synectics is based on the use of analogies.) One simply tries to relate an object, person, or situation to the original problem, developing new problem definitions for the analogies and then relating them back to the original problem. The Pringle's Potato Chip example illustrates the use of analogy in problem-finding. While the original problem might have been stated as, "In what ways might we package potato chips into a small area without crushing them?" the analogy with leaves might lead to the statement, "In what ways might we form potato chips into uniform shapes?"

Pareto analysis has become a popular tool for problem-finding, especially in quality assurance. This tool is named after Vilfredo Pareto (1848–1923), an Italian economist who determined that 85 percent of the world's wealth was owned by only 15 percent of the people. To apply Pareto analysis, we gather data (fact-finding!) on the frequency of various problems. Typically, only a few problems account for a large percentage of the total problems. In quality assurance, for example, we typically find that about 85 percent of the quality costs are caused by only 15 percent of the problems. (Joseph Juran calls these problems the "vital few," since solving them will have a significant impact on overall quality costs. The remaining 85 percent are called the "trivial many.")

Other techniques that have been advocated to aid in problem-finding are **dialectical inquiry** and **devil's advocacy**.[39] Dialectical inquiry was developed in the context of strategic planning. It begins by identifying the current or recommended strategic plan and the data used to derive it. Next, assumptions underlying the plan are identified. These assumptions are then challenged through a counterplan. A structured debate, in which forceful presentations of the two opposing plans are presented, is conducted. The purpose of the debate is to force the audience to focus on and evaluate the assumptions underlying each plan. This helps to develop new and better definitions of the underlying problems that the plans address. In the devil's advocate approach, another individual assumes the role of a critic of a plan. The plan's defects are discussed, and reasons are given why the plan should not be adopted. This process helps to deepen understanding and forms the basis for revised definitions.

Various other techniques have been proposed to aid the problem-finding effort in DS/MS situations. Among these are the use of computer models for problem identification,[40] simulation,[41] discussion of solutions[42] (this technique is similar to the "Ask Why?" approach found in the creative-thinking literature), and the use of gaming.[43]

Once a collection of tentative problem statements has been developed, the convergent phase of problem-finding aims to select the problem statement that best captures the "real" problem to be solved.

IDEA-FINDING

Idea-finding was the major focus of Chapter 3. Structured techniques such as brainstorming, forced relationships, attribute listing, and so forth provide stimulants for generating ideas for solutions. The more techniques that you can use to stimulate ideas, the more ideas you will be able to generate. As Woolsey stated, "I feel that one of our most important jobs is to 'provide creative alternatives.' "[44]

As with the other phases of creative problem solving, idea-finding is a divergent-convergent process. The divergent phase of idea-finding is simply to generate as many ideas as possible for solving the problem. The rules of brainstorming—don't criticize, strive for quantity, encourage freewheeling, and combine and recombine—should guide this process. As a first step, write down all the ideas that you can think of immediately. This helps to get the common and trivial ideas out of your mind. Then consider using some of the idea-stimulation methods from Chapter 3.

A powerful yet simple method to find ideas is to ask, "What if?" For instance, consider the foundry problem stated thus: "In what ways might we motivate the foundry to get more complete sets of parts to the finishing shop?" Some "what if" statements might be:

What if no partial sets could leave the foundry floor?
What if everyone could see the high level of partial inventory?
What if we do nothing?

After reviewing these statements, the following ideas might be suggested:

Direct the foundry manager not to move any incomplete sets to the holding
  warehouse.
Move the holding warehouse next to the foundry.
Put a sign in the foundry, where everyone could see it, stating the number
  or percentage of partial sets stored in the holding warehouse.
Revise (lengthen) customer delivery dates.

   Another method of generating ideas for solutions is to change the wording of the problem statement. Simple modification of a single word can dramatically change the meaning. For example, consider the statement, "In what ways might this company reduce quality costs by 30 percent?" Dropping the qualifier "by 30 percent" broadens the problem and the potential solutions. Relaxing the qualifier (such as "by 5 percent") produces a similar effect. Changing the action verb or goal can also change the problem perspective. For instance, changing "reduce" to "curtail" implies different possible solutions, such as eliminating quality training; changing "costs" to "problems" also makes a significant difference. One might also consider turning a negative statement into a positive one; for example, "reduce noise" to "increase quiet." A thesaurus is often invaluable in helping to redefine problem statements. One could write down lists of synonyms for the action verb or goal and try different combinations.
   Edward de Bono suggests a basic principle of problem redefinition analogous to Newton's second law of motion: For every well-defined direction of a problem, there will be an opposite and equally well-defined direction.[45] That is, **reverse** the direction of the problem (recall Osborn's checklist!) in any way possible and examine the new definitions that emerge. For example, consider the problem of "how to reduce costs due to excessive scrap." One way of reversing the direction of this statement would be to ask "how to use excessive scrap to reduce costs." This might suggest a new use of the scrap in packaging, for instance. Another reversal would be to change "reduce cost" to "increase revenues." This might suggest selling the scrap or using it to produce a new product.
   Brainstorming is often applied to develop a **cause-and-effect diagram**. A cause-and-effect diagram is a simple graphic method for presenting a chain of causes and effects and for organizing relationships among variables. Kaoru Ishikawa popularized cause-and-effect diagrams as a quality problem-solving tool in Japan. The general structure of a cause-and-effect diagram is shown in Figure 5-3. At the end of the horizontal line, a problem is listed. Each branch pointing into the main stem represents a possible cause. Branches pointing to the causes are contributors to these causes. An example is shown in Figure 5-4.

Figure 5-3 General Structure of a Cause-and-Effect Diagram

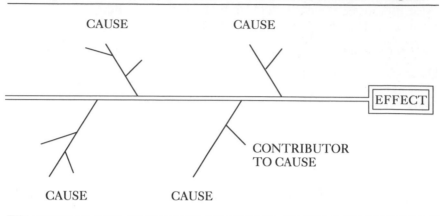

Figure 5-4 Example of a Cause-and-Effect Diagram

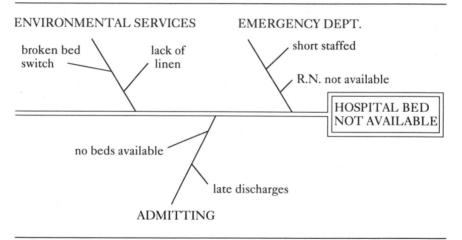

Problems in DS/MS often can be expressed by different representations. Rubinstein suggests that we should view the word *representation* as "re-presentation."[46] By re-presenting a problem in a different form, we may derive unique insights into the nature of the problem and, consequently, unique ideas for a solution. A good example of using graphic representation is the "Instant Insanity" puzzle.[47] Instant Insanity consists of four cubes, with each side painted in one of four colors. The problem is to arrange the cubes in a straight line so that one of each color shows on each of the four sides. Combinatorially, there are 41,472 possible arrangements of the cubes, but only one solution. By drawing a graphical representation of the problem, the solution can be easily found. This is given in Figure 5-5. Can you determine how to find the solution?

Figure 5-5 Graphic Representation of Instant Insanity

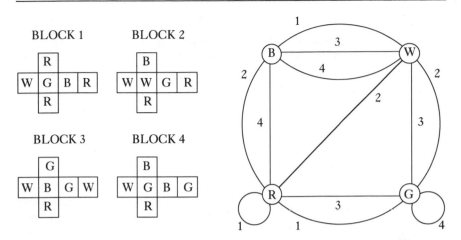

Note: Two colors are connected by a line if that block has these colors on opposite sides.

Developing problem formulations in management science involves a large amount of idea-generation. For example, determining what the variables should be and what constraints are relevant is an application of idea-finding. In a review of problem formulation in planning and design, Roger Volkema lists four factors that affect the amount of time and effort devoted to formulation of a problem.[48] These are (1) the complexities of the problem, (2) the capabilities and experiences of the planner or designer, (3) the environment in which the process takes place, and (4) the formulation process used by the planner or designer. Several decision strategies for reducing complexity in problem diagnosis and formulation are identified. Among these are several common creative-thinking enhancement techniques, such as morphological analysis and attribute listing. In addition, Volkema reported on an empirical study that showed that individuals with high creativity had a higher number of different solutions and better solution quality than individuals with low creativity. In the next chapter, we shall give some examples of how creative-thinking techniques can improve the DS/MS modeling effort.

In the convergent phase of idea-finding, one tries to narrow down the ideas to a smaller set of the best ideas. Use one or two of the most important criteria for screening—for example, the cost of the proposed solution or the time it would take to implement it—and eliminate those ideas that are clearly not feasible. In doing so, however, you run the risk of eliminating an idea that has the potential to be changed into a feasible alternative. Once a good set of ideas is agreed upon, you can proceed to the solution-finding phase.

SOLUTION-FINDING

Tentative solutions found in the idea-finding phase are usually rough and incomplete. The purpose of solution-finding is to evaluate potential solutions and develop them into useful actions for solving the problem. In solution-finding, divergence consists of generating criteria for screening and selecting ideas. Convergence is a two-part process. First you converge to screen and select the criteria; then converge to select a solution.

Criteria are objective standards that measure the value of potential solutions. Useful criteria usually include time, cost, acceptance, practicality, performance, and so on. The more criteria that we can develop to guide our judgment, the better we can evaluate our ideas. We should apply the principles of deferring judgment and producing quantity in developing the criteria themselves. We can then evaluate the criteria and select the most important ones. This reduces the chance of making the wrong decision because of inappropriate criteria. It also helps in anticipating problems that may hinder the acceptance of a solution. What criteria do you think are important to the foundry problem?

Using the foundry problem, we might evaluate the potential ideas as follows (what criteria are actually used here?):

1. Direct the foundry manager not to move any incomplete sets to the holding warehouse. If no partial sets could leave the foundry floor, workers would be unable to perform any new orders until the partial

sets are completed or moved out. However, priority jobs may be delayed while the low-priority jobs are completed just to get them out of the way.

2. Move the holding warehouse next to the foundry. The partial sets are no longer out of sight, but moving the warehouse will be expensive.

3. Put a sign in the foundry—where everyone (including the foundry workers and the plant manager) can see it—stating the number or percentage of partial sets stored in the holding warehouse. This shows top-management commitment and puts pressure on the foundry shop, but it may not have the impact of the other alternatives.

4. Revise (lengthen) customer delivery dates. This may alleviate the problem somewhat, but the firm might lose business.

As Woolsey states, "When you give the manager a spread of alternatives, with good points and bad points outlined, few can argue that the work is insufficient."[49] In the actual case, alternative three was chosen, but with a twist thrown in by the plant manager. He moved the foundry manager out of his air-conditioned office into the foundry, facing the sign. He suggested that he could move back in when there were consistently more parts in the completed-parts warehouse than in the other one. Needless to say, it did not take very long!

To evaluate more complex alternatives, decision-analytic methods and models are often used. Formal decision analysis methods such as decision trees are used to evaluate capacity expansion alternatives, and scoring models are frequently used to evaluate facility-location alternatives.[50] However, we must be cautious of model fixation and overmodeling.[51] Woolsey notes that common failures of mathematical programming are a result of failure of the modeler to realize that the method is a means to an end rather than an end itself, and extrapolating the wrong answer from the right method.[52] Models should be used to provide insight.[53]

Mulvey provides an excellent illustration of divergence-convergence in model selection for a personnel-scheduling problem, which we introduced in Chapter 3.[54] Five criteria for model assessment were proposed: performance, realism/complexity, information requirements, user friendliness, and computational costs. The three models were evaluated along these dimensions before selection. Similar evaluation processes have been advocated for selecting heuristics.[55]

Other examples of creativity in solution-finding can be found in many of Gene Woolsey's anecdotes.[56]

ACCEPTANCE-FINDING

Acceptance-finding is the final phase in the creative problem solving process. In acceptance-finding, one develops a plan of action to implement the solution. Acceptance must be gained from oneself, as well as from others. Often, one must sell the solution to the client. It not unusual to find that solutions need to be modified to address implementation problems. We need to prepare for any problems that might arise in implementing ideas.

VanGundy presents a checklist of questions to ask that could affect the implementation of a solution:[57]

1. Are resources (time, personnel, equipment, money, information, and so on) adequate for implementing this idea?
2. Do others possess the motivation and commitment needed for successful implementation?
3. Is the idea likely to encounter "closed thinking" and/or resistance to change in general?
4. Are there procedural obstacles that need to be overcome?
5. Are there structural obstacles in the organization that need to be overcome (e.g., communication channels that might block implementation)?
6. What organizational or managerial policies will need to be overcome?
7. How much risk taking is likely to be tolerated by those responsible for implementation?
8. Are there any ongoing power struggles within the organization—even if unrelated to the idea—that might block implementation?
9. Are there any interpersonal conflicts that might prevent or hinder the idea from being put into action?
10. Is the general climate of the organization one of cooperation or distrust?

Isaksen and Treffinger suggest first generating a list of assisters and resisters, namely those respective factors that can help gain acceptance of the solution or hinder its acceptance.[58] This is the divergent phase of the step. As before, we wish to strive for quantity; thus, we must identify as many factors as possible. The same information-gathering processes used in fact-finding can be used—for example, asking who? what? when? where? why? and how? After these have been identified, one converges, looking for commonalities and reducing the list to smaller groups. This is followed by the development of an action plan that details who will perform various activities—and when, where, and how. Other formal techniques, such as Kepner-Tregoe Potential Problem Analysis and PERT/CPM, can be used in the acceptance-finding phase.[59]

As noted in Chapter 2, Woolsey suggests that clients can be motivated to use DS/MS models because of (1) desire for status, (2) greed, and (3) fear. Hence, the first question that an analyst should ask (putting himself or herself in the client's shoes) is, "What's in it for me?" The answer must be available in terms that the decision maker can understand. My favorite "creative" example of acceptance-finding involves a South American company whose tool crib was presided over by Octaviano Huerta, who was within two years of retirement.[60] Over the years, the tool-inventory paperwork system had deteriorated and was no longer used; Octaviano relied on his memory to fill out weekly totals to the accounting department. To reduce tool losses, management wanted the record keeping to be maintained accurately. While Octaviano was agreeable, he pointed out that he had been trying for years to get the men to fill out the forms, but with no success (and with threats of bodily harm from one Mr. Oso).

Octaviano was offered the following deal. For every end-of-month inventory count that matched exactly with the pull tickets, he would be given one-half of one percent of the value of the tool crib (which was over $300,000). Woolsey's tale of Octaviano's "acceptance-finding" procedure goes as follows:

Oso: "Give me one of these!"

Huerta: "Certainly, but first we have a new system in force, you must fill out the form."

Oso: "I have never done it before and I won't do it now, give me the tool."

Huerta: "Not until you fill out the form."

Oso: "Perhaps, old man, your memory has failed you as to the result of our last conversation on this subject. GIVE ME THE TOOL!"

Huerta: "Fill out the *form!*"

Oso: (leaning over the half-door) "If you don't give me the tool *right now* I am going to tear off this door and make you *eat it.*"

(At this point reliable witnesses agree that, shaking visibly, Huerta reached under the half-door and produced, holding it with both hands, a cocked single-action .44, shoved it into Oso's gut, and said softly, but firmly:)

Huerta: "Fill out the form?"

To which Oso replied:

Oso: "Si, comprendo."

Of all the steps in the creative problem-solving process, implementation has probably generated the most attention in the DS/MS literature.[61] Meredith classifies implementation failure into three diverse sets of factors: technical (those factors related primarily to the mechanics of implementation), process (those factors concerned with system initiation and use), and inner-environmental (those related to the organization's internal environment).[62] Understanding these issues is critical in acceptance-finding.

Evidence exists that increased creativity can reduce implementation problems in DS/MS. It has been observed that interface facilities between analytical systems and users are critical; users want complex models that are easy to use.[63] One key factor in successful implementation is the user's participation in defining the problem.[64] In a survey conducted by Watson and Marett, a major conclusion was that management scientists do not understand the needs of management.[65] This implies that more attention must be paid to the mess-finding, fact-finding, and problem-finding phases of the process.

Some authors question whether DS/MS failure is indeed due to implementation and implicitly suggest that more creativity is needed in modeling.[66]
The following questions are suggested:

1. Have we left out important goals of the decision maker (mess-
   finding)?
2. Perhaps our criteria are wrong. Do we force artificial criteria onto
   problems so that our models will work (fact-finding and problem-
   finding)?
3. Are our models deficient (idea-finding)?
4. Should we try to optimize in the traditional sense (solution-finding)?

CONCLUSION

In reviewing the six steps of the creative problem-solving process and
their relationships to DS/MS, a significant opportunity exists to improve DS/
MS methodology and problem solving by focusing more attention on divergent
thinking. This opens up several avenues for new empirical research. In the
next chapter we propose and illustrate a simple integrated framework that
combines both processes.

Treffinger and Huber propose a set of learning objectives for instruction
in creative problem solving.[67] These can easily be classified according to the
Osborn/Parnes process:

1. **Mess-Finding**. Be sensitive to problems and be able to describe the
   many specific problems from a mess that could be appropriately
   attacked; articulate many elements of the situation; and employ a
   checklist of elements to extend an analysis of possible problems.
2. **Fact-Finding**. Be able to observe carefully and discover facts by
   listing many attributes or characteristics of the situation, describing
   factors that may influence observation; state the difficulties associated
   with "shifting one's viewpoint"; describe several techniques for
   breaking the limiting mindset resulting from past experience; and
   describe the features, characteristics, and functions of the important
   parts of the situation.
3. **Problem-Finding**. Be able to recognize the "hidden" or "real"
   problem that may underlie the mess; broaden the problem; clarify
   and redefine it; and identify several subproblems that are more man-
   ageable or that can be more easily solved because they are more
   clearly defined.
4. **Idea-Finding**. Be able to use several techniques for facilitating idea
   production; demonstrate the use of Osborn's "idea-spurring questions" list to generate new ideas; and demonstrate the use of analogies in finding useful ideas.

5. **Solution-Finding**. Be able to demonstrate ways in which "silly" ideas can be made useful; describe the problems associated with vague criteria; demonstrate techniques for rating ideas and working first with the most important ideas; identify a variety of criteria for evaluating alternatives; develop many criteria for any problem; and demonstrate deferring of judgment with respect to criteria.

6. **Acceptance-Finding**. Be able to plan for the implementation of ideas by identifying specific sources of difficulty in implementing them; demonstrating the use of implementation check lists, key word lists, and implementation stimulators to recognize and overcome possible blocks to implementation; and specifying a plan for facilitating implementation and acceptance.

EXERCISES

1.   Describe personal experiences in which you have had an "Aha!" experience after some period of incubation.

2.   A speaker arrived to give a talk at a meeting and noticed that no lectern had been provided. She defined her problem as, "Where might I get a lectern in a hurry?" What was her *real* problem?[68]

3.   What characteristics of creative individuals do you feel are the most important in helping identify messes?

4.   How many triangles do you see in the following:

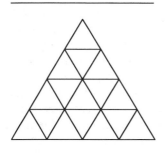

Of what value is this exercise?

5.   **The Staffing Problem:**[69] In the geriatric ward of a hospital, which houses about 20 patients, the staff are concerned about patients who wander into rooms of other patients and cause a disturbance. At any one time there seem to be three to four patients who have difficulty finding their rooms. One of the hospital's administrators has suggested

that the patients be escorted back to their rooms. However, this would require that some time be freed up for an already overworked staff. As an assistant to the administrator, you are asked to come up with a plan to free up staff time. You must present the plan at the next administrative meeting. How would you approach this situation?

6. Use the "why" technique to redefine the following problems:
   a. In what ways might I (IWWMI) receive an "A" in this course?
   b. IWWMI find a spouse?
   c. IWWMI find the money to buy a sportscar?
   d. IWWMI be elected president of my fraternity or professional society?
   e. IWWMI open the lid on this jar?
   f. IWWMI get my subordinates to do their jobs effectively?
   g. IWWMI get admitted to graduate school?

7. List criteria for
   a. evaluating the choice of a graduate school
   b. selecting among competing job offers
   c. buying a car
   d. selecting a husband/wife

8. Your fraternity or professional society has committed itself to hosting a major regional conference. You are the chairperson responsible for coordinating all the volunteer help. As the deadlines approach, very little has been done. You see the problem as being, "How do we get the volunteers to carry out their tasks?" Propose solutions, evaluate them, and develop an implementation plan.

9. Use Osborn's checklist to propose other means of redefining problems, similarly to the use of reversal as discussed in the chapter.

ENDNOTES

1. Further historical notes and comments can be found in Arthur B. VanGundy, *Creative Problem Solving: A Guide for Trainers and Management* (New York: Quorum Books, 1987), and John W. Haefele, *Creativity and Innovation* (New York: Reinhold, 1962).

2. J. Dewey, *How We Think* (New York: D.C. Heath, 1933).

3. J.H. McPherson, "The People, The Problems and the Problem-Solving Methods," *Journal of Creative Behavior* 2, no. 2 (1968): pp. 103–110.

4. S.J. Parnes, R.B. Noller, and A.M. Biondi, eds., *Guide to Creative Action* (New York: Charles Scribner's Sons, 1977).

5. Russell L. Ackoff, "Beyond Problem Solving," *Decision Sciences* 5, no. 2: pp. x–xv.

6. Colin Eden, "Problem Construction and the Influence of O.R.," *Interfaces* 12, no. 2: pp. 50–60.

7. Gene Woolsey, "Two Essays on Model Motivation: With This Sign, Optimize & The Shekels of Silver Solution," *Interfaces* vol. 9, no. 1 (1978): pp. 13–17.

8. Samuel J. Mantel, Jr., private communication.

9. See Charles Schwenk and Howard Thomas, "Formulating the Mess: The Role of Decision Aids in Problem Formulation," *OMEGA, The International Journal of Management Science* 11, no. 3 (1983): pp. 239–62.

10. William F. Pounds, "The Process of Problem Finding," *Industrial Management Review* 11, no. 4 (1969): pp. 1–19. The literature often uses the terms "problem finding" or "problem identification" to mean what we call mess-finding. The reader needs to be aware of the subtle differences.

11. David A. Cowan, "Developing a Process Model of Problem Recognition," *Academy of Management Review* 11, no. 4 (1986): pp. 763–76.

12. G.F. Smith, "Managerial Problem Identification," *OMEGA, The International Journal of Management Science* 17, no. 1 (1989): pp. 27–36. This paper also reports on an empirical research study designed to validate claims made in prior research.

13. See Ronald N. Taylor, "Perception of Problem Constraints," *Management Science* 22, no. 1: pp. 22–29 and Robert J. Graham and Mohammad Jahani, "People, Problems and Planning: A Systems Approach to Problem Identification," *Interfaces* 8, no. 1 (November 1977): pp. 50–53, for discussions of this idea.

14. VanGundy, *Creative Problem Solving.*

15. Graham and Jahani, "People, Problems, and Planning."

16. This discussion is adapted from Gordon Raisbeck, "How the Choice of Measures of Effectiveness Constrains Operational Analysis," *Interfaces* 9, no. 4 (August 1979): pp. 85–93. This paper presents several examples of public sector and defense applications of measures of effectiveness, particularly focusing on errors resulting from poor choices.

17. Glen L. Urban, "Building Models for Decision Makers," *Interfaces* 4, no. 3 (May 1974): pp. 1–11.

18. VanGundy, *Creative Problem Solving.*

19. Woolsey, "Two Essay."

20. M. Pidd and R.N. Woolley, "Four Views on Problem Structuring," *Interfaces* 10, no. 1 (February 1980): pp. 51–54.

21. C.H. Kepner and B.B Tregoe, *The Rational Manager* (New York: McGraw-Hill, 1965). Harvey Brightman also provides a good discussion of this approach in *Group Problem Solving: An Improved Managerial Approach* (Atlanta, GA: Business Publishing Division, Georgia State University, 1988).

22. Patrick Rivett, *Principles of Model Building* (London: John Wiley & Sons, 1972),

devotes an entire chapter (chapter 5) to accounting data. Many of Woolsey's anecdotes revolve around the role of accounting data in fact-finding. In particular, see "The Measure of M.S./O.R. Applications, or Let's Hear It for the Bean Counters," *Interfaces* 5, no. 2 (1975): pp. 74–78, and "Walking Thru Warehouses, Tool Cribs & Shops or Profits Thru Peripatetics," *Interfaces* 8, no. 2 (1978): pp. 15–20.

23. Robert J. Graham, "'Give the Kid a Number': An Essay on the Folly and Consequences of Trusting Your Data," *Interfaces* 12, no. 2 (1982): pp. 40-44.

24. Woolsey, "Walking Through Warehouses," pp. 15–19.

25. Two good references that discuss analytical methods for systems analysis and evaluation are Andrew P. Sage, *Methodology for Large Scale Systems* (New York: McGraw-Hill, 1977), and Van Court Hare, Jr., *Systems Analysis: A Diagnostic Approach* (New York: Harcourt, Brace & World, 1967).

26. Robert E.D. Woolsey, "The Fifth Column: On Inventory System Incentives, or The Case of the Overbought Antifreeze," *Interfaces* 18, no. 6 (November-December 1988) pp. 23–27. Many of Woolsey's other articles deal with similar issues of fact-finding, which often boils down to "doing dumb things first." A recurring theme in many of them is that once the appropriate facts are discovered, the real problems and solutions are often incredibly easy to find.

27. Schwenk and Thomas, "Formulating the Mess," pp. 239–52.

28. Early empirical research investigating the relationship between problem statements and solution options has been described by K. Kunckner, "On Problem Solving," *Psychological Monographs* 58, no. 5 (1945): p. 270; A.I. Judson and C.N. Cofer, "Reasoning as an Associative Process: I. Direction in a Simple Verbal Problem," *Psychological Reports* 2 (1956): pp. 469–476; and N.R.F. Maier and R.J. Burke, "Response Availability as a Factor in the Problem-Solving Performance of Males and Females," *Journal of Personality and Social Psychology* 5 (1967): pp. 304–310. Roger J. Volkema provides a comprehensive review of problem statements, focusing on research issues, in "Problem Statements in Managerial Problem Solving," *Socio-Economic Planning Sciences* 22, no. 5 (1988): pp. 213–20.

29. P.F. Drucker, *The Practice of Management* (New York: Harper and Row, 1954), pp. 352–53.

30. J.T. Dillon, "Problem Finding and Solving," *Journal of Creative Behavior* 16, no. 2 (1982): pp. 97–111.

31. Other good examples of problem-finding can be found in Woolsey's article "The Fifth Column: Sales Psychology of MS/MIS Systems: Why Some Work, Why Some Win," *Interfaces* 19, no. 2 (March-April 1989): pp. 29–33. An excellent case study involving a university library is reported in R.S. Stainton, "Pathways to Solutions," *OMEGA: The International Journal of Management Science* 12, no. 1 (1984): pp. 11–18. Stainton observes that the order in which facts are collected, the attitudes of people involved in the problem, and the climate in which the problem finds itself all play roles in determining what the problem is perceived to be and how it is tackled.

32. Ian Mitroff and I. Featheringham, "On Systematic Problem Solving and the Error of the Third Kind," *Behavioral Science* 19, no. 6 (1974): pp. 383–93. Also, see Surya B. Yadav and Apparao Korukonda, "Management of Type III Error in Problem Identification," *Interfaces* 15, no. 4 (1985): 55–61. This paper presents a case study of type III errors that occurred in the start-up and operation of a chemical plant.

33. "Secret to Perfect Kernels Might Be Just a Pop Away," *The Cincinnati Enquirer*, November 7, 1989, p. A-2.

34. S.G. Isaksen and D.J. Treffinger, *Creative Problem Solving: The Basic Course* (Buffalo, NY: Bearly, 1985). Isaksen and Treffinger proposed the first three components; VanGundy (*Creative Problem Solving*) added the goal component. Volkema, "Problem Statement," discusses other forms of problem statements.

35. VanGundy, *Creative Problem Solving*.

36. M.A. Lyles and I.I. Mitroff, "Organizational Problem Formulation: An Empirical Study," *Administrative Science Quarterly* 25, no. 1: pp. 102–119.

37. Volkema, Roger J., "Problem Formulation in Planning and Design," *Management Science* 29, no. 6: pp. 639–52.

38. The creative solution to this problem was to install mirrors to eliminate the perception of waiting.

39. See Schwenk and Thomas, "Formulating the Mess." This paper provides a comprehensive literature review of decision aids in problem formulation (including creativity stimulants).

40. Robert J. Graham, "Problem and Opportunity Identification in Management Science," *Interfaces* 6, no. 4 (1976): pp. 79–82.

41. Suraj M. Alexander, "Discovering and Correcting Problems in a Naval Stock Control System," *Interfaces* 15, no. 4 (1985): pp. 41–47.

42. Robert J. Graham, "The Use of 'Solutions' for Problem Identification," *Interfaces* 7, no. 1 (1976): pp. 63–65.

43. Laurence D. Richards and Robert J. Graham, "Identifying Problems through Gaming," *Interfaces* 7, no. 3: pp. 76–83.

44. Woolsey, "Two Essays."

45. Edward de Bono, *Lateral Thinking: Creativity Step By Step* (New York: Harper & Row, 1970).

46. Moshe F. Rubinstein, *Tools for Thinking and Problem Solving*, (Englewood Cliffs, NJ: Prentice-Hall, 1986), p. 6.

47. To my knowledge, this graphic solution was first proposed by Saaty in *Topics in Behavioral Mathematics* (Mathematical Association of America, 1973), pp. 45–47.

48. Volkema, "Problem Formulation," pp. 639–52.

49. Woolsey, "Two Essays."

50.   See, for example, James R. Evans et al., *Applied Production and Operations Management*, 3d ed. (St. Paul, MN: West Publishing, 1990). This book provides several examples of the use of decision analysis techniques and scoring models in P/OM situations.

51.   Harvey N. Shycon presents a case study to this effect in "All Around the Model: Perspectives on MS Applications," *Interfaces* 4, no. 3 (May 1974): pp. 23–25.

52.   R.E.D. Woolsey, "A Novena to St. Jude, or Four Edifying Case Studies in Mathematical Programming," *Interfaces* 4, no. 1: pp. 48–52.

53.   See R.E.D. Woolsey, "A Candle to St. Jude, or Four Real World Applications of Integer Programming," *Interfaces* 2, no. 2 (1972): pp. 20–27, and Allen F. Grum and Rick Hesse, "It's the Process Not the Product (Most of the Time)," *Interfaces* 13, no. 5 (1983): pp. 89–93, for further discussions of this theme.

54.   John M. Mulvey, "Strategies in Modeling: A Personnel Scheduling Example," *Interfaces* 9, no. 3 (1979): pp. 66–77.

55.   Stelios H. Zanakis and James R. Evans, "Heuristic 'Optimization': Why, When, and How to Use It," *Interfaces* 11, no. 5, (October 1981): pp. 84–91.

56.   In particular, see the following: "A Candle to St. Jude, or Four Real World Applications of Integer Programming," *Interfaces* 2, no. 2 (1972): pp. 20–27; "A Novena to St. Jude, or Four Edifying Case Studies in Mathematical Programming," *Interfaces* 4, no. 1 (1973): pp. 32–39; "Two Digressions on Systems Analysis: Optimum Warehousing & Disappearing Orange Juice," *Interfaces* 7, no. 2 (1977): pp. 17–20; "Walking Thru Warehouses, Tool Cribs & Shops or Profits Thru Peripatetics," *Interfaces* 8, no. 2 (1978): pp. 15-20; "Neither a Borrower Nor a Lender Be, or The Bank Shot Revisited," *Interfaces* 10, no. 3 (1980): pp. 9–11; "The Dispatch Model That Was Too Simple, or What the Feds Don't Know Can't Hurt 'Em," *Interfaces* 13, no. 1 (1983): pp. 76–78; and "On the Proper Scheduling of the Vampires, or Phlebotomy Follies," *Interfaces* 13, no. 3 (1983): pp. 72–74. As an exercise, you might wish to do an analysis of the creativity of the *titles* of his papers!

57.   VanGundy, *Techniques of Structured Problem Solving*, p. 190.

58.   Isaksen and Treffinger, *Creative Problem Solving*.

59.   See VanGundy, *Creative Problem Solving*, for detailed discussions of these techniques.

60.   Gene Woolsey, "An Essay in the Management of Inventory, or Por Razon Si Possible, Por Fuerza Si Necessario!" *Interfaces* 12, no. 3 (June, 1982), pp. 10–21. The reader is urged to study two other interesting examples of acceptance-finding by Woolsey: "A Case of Optimum Trucking, or To Keep on Rising, Just Keep on Truckin'," *Interfaces* 8, no. 1 (November 1977), pp. 12–15, and "The Fifth Column: On System Acceptance," *Interfaces* 16, no. 3 (May-June 1986): pp. 55–59.

61.   See, for instance, A.G. Lockett and E. Polding, "OR/MS Implementation—A Variety of Processes," *Interfaces* 9, no. 1 (1978): pp. 45–50. The May-June 1987

(vol. 17, no. 3) issue of *Interfaces* is devoted exclusively to implementation papers. This is an excellent starting point to begin a study of this topic.

62. Jack Meredith, "The Importance of Impediments to Implementation," *Interfaces* 11, no. 4 (1981): pp. 71–74.

63. R.F. Powers, J.J. Darrenbauer, and George Doolittle, "The Myth of the Simple Model," *Interfaces* 13, no. 6 (1983): pp. 84–91.

64. Lars Lonnstedt, "Factors Related to the Implementation of Operations Research Solutions," *Interfaces* 9, no. 1: pp. 45–50.

65. Hugh J. Watson and Particia Gill Marett, "A Survey of Management Science Implementation Problems," *Interfaces* 9, no. 4 (1979): pp. 124–28.

66. Richard F. Barton, "Models With More Than One Criterion—Or Why Not Build Implementation Into the Model?" *Interfaces* 7, no. 4 (1977): pp. 71–75.

67. D. Treffinger and J. Huber, "Designing Instruction in Creative Problem-Solving: Preliminary Objectives and Learning Hierarchies," *Journal of Creative Behavior* 9 (1975): pp. 260–66.

68. Adapted from Parnes, Noller, and Biondi, *Guide to Creative Action*, pp. 319–20.

69. Adapted from Volkema, "Problem Formulation," p. 650.

CHAPTER 6
Management Science, Modeling, and Creative Thinking

INTRODUCTION

The Osborn/Parnes creative problem-solving (CPS) process that we presented and discussed in the last chapter provides a structured approach for addressing *any* problem. This might be a personal problem, a behavioral problem, or an operational problem that requires an analytical approach. We have deliberately avoided discussions of problem solving using mathematical models to emphasize the generality of creative problem solving in DS/MS. Our major focus in this chapter is to examine the role of CPS within the framework of quantitative modeling. CPS does not replace traditional methodology but enriches it. We conclude this chapter by discussing the development of creativity for decision and management scientists.

OPERATIONS RESEARCH METHODOLOGY AND THE CPS PROCESS

VanGundy describes four major components common to all problem-solving processes:[1]

1. redefining and analyzing the problem

2. generating ideas
3. evaluating and selecting ideas
4. implementing ideas

Redefinition and analysis are the collection and organization of information, analysis of data and underlying assumptions, and a "twisting" of the problem to examine new perspectives. The goal is to achieve a workable problem definition. Idea generation simply develops as many solutions as possible. Evaluation and selection are activities whose goal is to produce a useful solution. It should be obvious that the Osborn/Parnes CPS involves these components. For example, mess-finding, fact-finding, and problem-finding are concerned with redefinition and analysis; idea-finding stands alone; solution-finding evaluates and selects ideas; and acceptance-finding focuses on implementation.

The classic operations research methodology can be stated as follows:[2]

1. Problem formulation
2. Model construction
3. Solution derivation
4. Model and solution testing
5. Establishment of controls
6. Putting the solution to work

Problem formulation involves an analysis of the system under study, the objectives of the decision-maker, and alternative courses of action. With a model in mind, this step results in the selection of decision variables, uncontrollable variables, constraints, and objectives. It is easy to see that this step involves elements of mess-finding, fact-finding, and problem-finding; in short, redefinition and analysis. Model construction consists of finding relationships among the controllable and uncontrollable variables, resulting in an objective function and constraint functions. Solution derivation involves the choice of a particular technique or algorithm for solving the model. Idea generation is fundamental to both the construction and solution of the model, but it is notably lacking in the formal description of the methodology. Model and solution testing involve

1. determining the predictive ability of the model,
2. verifying the data, and
3. validating the relationships expressed in the model.

Establishment of controls means developing ranges about the solution and developing rules for modifying the solution when changes occur. This step—and actually putting the solution to work—comprise implementation.

VanGundy's observations provide a convenient link between the classic operations research methodology and the creative problem-solving process. We illustrate this in Figure 6–1.

The framework in Figure 6–1 illustrates that the operations research problem-solving process as a whole follows a sequence of steps similar to the

**Figure 6–1 Relationships Between Creative Problem Solving
and Operations Research Methodology**

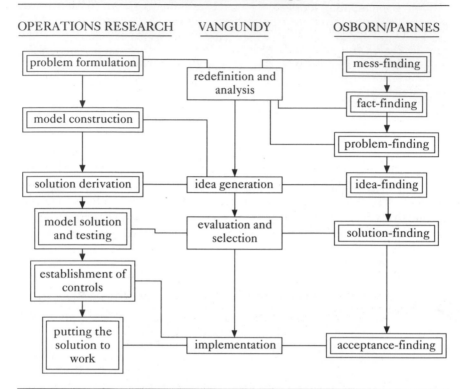

general creative problem-solving process. We must, however, recognize that
each step of the O.R. process is focused on a specific result. For example,
the goal of "problem formulation" is to derive a statement of the decision
variables, uncontrollable variables, constraints, and objectives. Typically, one
must

1. understand the nature of the mess to formulate the problem;
2. find facts, such as the uncontrollable factors and environmental con-
    ditions surrounding the mess;
3. identify the true problem; generate ideas for the decision variables,
    constraints, and objectives;
4. determine the best set of variables, constraints, and objectives (that
    is, find a "solution" to the formulation problem); and
5. guarantee that the formulation indeed addresses the decision maker's
    problem (i.e., acceptance-finding).

We see that *we need to work through each step in the CPS process* to develop a
good problem formulation.

The model construction phase is similar. We begin with a mess—the problem formulation; find facts (Are the relationships linear? Are there any stochastic elements? What are the costs of collecting the data? What software is available?); determine the true problem (What will the model be used for? How much reality is necessary in the model? How accurate should the model be?); generate ideas for expressing the problem statement mathematically (What alternate model representations can be used? What approximation or aggregation schemes might be useful?); evaluate and select the best model; and plan for implementation (Do we have the software or technology to solve it? In what form should the solution be presented to the user?). Again, there is a need to consider each step of the CPS process to develop a good model.

Thus, we see that problem formulation itself is a mess to be resolved. Model construction is also a mess to be resolved. In fact, *each step* of the operations research process can be viewed as taking the result created in the previous step, treating it as a new mess, and resolving it. Thus, we are suggesting that CPS can be used to *improve* one's ability to solve problems using the traditional operations research methodology by applying the CPS process to each step. Figure 6–2 presents a conceptual model for describing this

Figure 6–2 A Framework for a Creative Operations Research Methodology

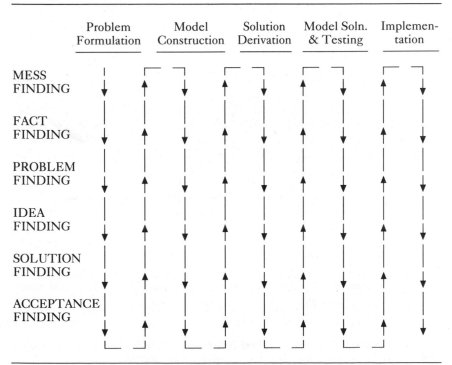

process. Brightman has discussed similar ideas in the context of Simon's three-phase model of intelligence, design, and choice.[3]

Below we shall present an example of how the CPS process can be applied to the problem-formulation step of the operations research methodology.

Applying CPS to Problem Formulation: Snow and Ice Control[4]

Mess-finding

I received a call from the facility and fleet manager in the engineer's office of a midsized county. He had received an MBA, taken a course in management science, and was convinced there was a better way to route the salt truck and snow plows in the county. He was on the verge of purchasing new trucks because the current fleet was unable to meet demand adequately. At $75,000 a truck, this was an important problem. Since vehicle routing problems are common in management science, I knew that some mathematical/computer model probably could improve the existing situation. However, the first step was to develop a problem formulation from this "mess."

Fact-finding

In an interview with the manager, he revealed that the county had 12 trucks that were dispatched from a central location and assigned to 12 routes. These routes were formed after geographically partitioning the county into 12 regions. Some trucks, however, could not salt their entire route in one load but had to return to the salt depot to refill. Data on the road network, truck capacities, salting rates, average vehicle speeds, and so forth were readily available.

Problem-finding

Several problems, or more specifically, solutions, were suggested during the fact-finding phase. Among these were:

1. In what ways can we keep critical road segments clear by rush hour?
2. In what ways can we revise routing plans for contingencies (breakdowns in equipment and so forth)?
3. In what ways can we perform "what if" analyses considering a possible remote salt depot?
4. How many trucks should be purchased?

We decided to concentrate initially on a simple system for routing a fleet of trucks efficiently, ignoring multiple salt depots or issues related to the timing of truck dispatching to salt critical road segments by rush hour. Such a system would allow the comparison of the existing route structure with new computer-generated routes and investigate the implications of different vehicle fleet mixes.

Idea-finding

Several ideas for formulating this problem were generated. Performance measures that were considered included minimizing the amount of deadheading (time on the route not spent productively salting or plowing), minimizing the total distance travelled on all routes, and minimizing the time to salt all roads (i.e., the time that the last road is salted by some truck). Obvious constraints were that no vehicle capacity could be exceeded on any route and that all roads had to be salted. Another constraint might have been to place an upper limit on the time permitted to salt all roads (as opposed to including this factor as an objective). The number of trucks and their capacities were an obvious constraint. However, another idea was to leave this unknown and to let the system determine the number and type of vehicles necessary to meet the other criteria. This led to the number and type of trucks becoming decision variables. Other decision variables were the actual routes taken and the salt rate (pounds per lane-mile).

Solution-finding

To make the system flexible, we decided to consider more than one problem formulation in designing the system. One principal formulation was to determine routes to minimize deadheading, given a fixed fleet of vehicles and an option to specify the maximum time allowed to salt all routes. A second formulation was to determine routes and vehicle capacities to minimize the number of vehicles required to meet a maximum time constraint.

Acceptance-finding

This was accomplished through agreement with the facility and fleet manager. The problems of multiple depots and dispatch timing were to be considered later if necessary, after the basic system was developed. In late summer, a dry run was performed using the new routes. The drivers liked the new routes, and only minor fine-tuning of the model parameters was necessary. The acid test came in November of that year, when a major snow storm hit. The predicted times of the new routes were off by only a few percent from the actual times observed.

Postscript

We focused the model construction phase on designing heuristic optimization algorithms for meeting the objectives and constraints defined in the problem formulations. This project resulted in a software package called

SnowMaster, which is marketed to state, county, and municipal governments. In the original application, the software generated savings of over $250,000 in capital equipment. (Instead of buying additional vehicles, it was shown that at least three vehicles could be eliminated!). Additional savings in labor, fuel, and other operating expenses also resulted.

CREATIVE THINKING IN MODELING

A modeler must make several important decisions:[5]

1. To what extent should reality be captured in the model?
2. How accurate should the model be?
3. What type of algorithm should be used?
4. What type of computer and software or programming language should be employed, if any?

The purpose of modeling is to gain insight from reality. Benefits accrue from (a) the quality of the solution and (b) the ease of understanding the solution process. John Little has suggested that models should be understandable, complete, evolutionary, easy to control, easy to communicate with, robust, and adaptive.[6]

Model-building is very much an art, and as such, requires a significant amount of creativity. William Morris has provided one of the few discussions of this aspect of modeling.[7] Morris observes that the modeling process is best described as intuitive, meaning that the thought process behind it cannot be verbalized easily. It is interesting to note that Morris cites several papers and books relating to creativity that address developing this "intuition." While he does not propose a recipe for building models, he does suggest ideas that are related to creativity enhancement as discussed in Chapter 3.

Morris proposes three fundamental ideas:

1. Modeling may be viewed as a process of **enrichment** or **elaboration**. That is, one begins with simple models, often quite different from reality, and moves toward more elaborate models that capture the complexity of the real situation.[8]
2. **Analogy** or **association** with previously developed models plays an important role in the determination of the starting point of this process of enrichment or elaboration. We have discussed the role of analogy in creative thinking several times throughout this book. Classification schemes discussed in Chapter 1 provide crude analogies for suggesting model types. Research has shown that with simple linear programming problems, experienced modelers first attempt to classify the problem into a familiar situation, such as a product-mix

problem, a transportation problem, and so on. The more important issue is how to proceed from the discovery of an analogy or what to do if none appears possible.

3. The process of elaboration or enrichment involves at least two sorts of **looping** or **alternation** procedures:

   a. The alternation between modification of the model and confrontation by the data. As each version of the model is tested, a new version is produced, which leads to a new test.

   b. The alternation between the tractability (ease of solution) of the model and the complexity of the model assumptions. If the model is tractable, the modeler may seek to enrich it further; if not, the modeler might simplify the assumptions to make it tractable.

Morris presents a checklist of ideas for improving the modeling process:

1. Factor the system problem into simpler problems. (We did this in formulating the snow-and-ice control problem.)
2. Establish a clear statement of deductive objectives. What do we want the model to do—predict, optimize, or evaluate?
3. Seek analogies.
4. Consider a case of the problem with real numbers. This will clarify assumptions that characterize the example. Also, if this case of the problem can be solved easily, then perhaps the general problem also can be solved easily. Finally, a specific instance provides a starting point for defining variables and constraints symbolically, if needed.
5. Establish some symbols.
6. Write down the obvious, such as conservation laws, input-output relations, assumptions, and other common sense assumptions.
7. If a tractable model is obtained, enrich it (if necessary). Otherwise, simplify it. We may enrich models by making constants into variables, adding variables, using nonlinear relations, relaxing assumptions and restrictions, and adding stochastic components. Simplification involves just the opposite.

These suggestions, with a little reorganization, easily can be cast within the creative problem-solving framework:

1. Mess-finding: Establish a clear statement of deductive objectives.
2. Fact-finding: Write down the obvious.
3. Problem-finding: Factor the system problem into simpler problems.
4. Idea-finding: Seek analogies; write down a specific numerical instance of the problem.
5. Solution-finding: Establish some symbols.
6. Acceptance-finding: If the model is tractable, enrich it if necessary. Otherwise, simplify.

The checklist for enrichment and simplification can also be seen to be a subset of Osborn's checklist:

making constants into variables—modify
adding variables—magnify
using nonlinear relations—substitute
relaxing assumptions and restrictions—modify
adding stochastic components—magnify

We could certainly add the other components of Osborn's list: put to other uses (seek analogies); adapt (develop a "near analogy" into an accurate and useful model); minify (aggregate variables); rearrange (rearrange constraints in a Lagrangian function); reverse (make objectives into constraints or constraints into objectives); and combine (combine elements of different models, as we shall see in the example that follows).

Other creativity stimulants can assist in the modeling process. For example, attribute listing can provide a modeler with a set of basic facts that one may enrich or simplify. Morphological analysis can provide a framework for generating many alternative models to consider. Exercises at the end of this chapter will focus on these ideas. We now provide an example of using the CPS framework for model construction.

Applying the CPS Process to Model Construction: A Linear Programming Example

Consider the following problem (adopted from the test bank to Anderson et al.:[9])

A coffee manufacturer produces three blends of coffee: A, B, and C. Two types of beans are used in each blend: Colombian and Mexican. The percent composition of these two beans in each blend and the selling prices of each blend are given below.

Blend	Colombian	Mexican	Price
A	75	25	$2.70
B	45	55	2.30
C	35	65	2.45

The company has purchased 25,000 lbs. and 35,000 lbs. of Colombian and Mexican beans, respectively. Production costs are $1.10 per pound for each of the blends.

While this is a simple textbook problem, we shall use it to illustrate the importance of creative thinking. You might be surprised to see how such a simple problem can lead to a wide variety of perspectives.

Mess-finding

The mess is simply the verbal statement of the problem. Objectives are not clear, nor are the best means of defining variables.

Fact-finding

Fact-finding consists of extracting and classifying unknowns and parameters from the problem statement; for example:

- quantity of each blend to produce
- amount of each bean to use
- quantity of each bean in each blend
- price
- percent composition
- pounds of each bean available
- production cost

Problem-finding

We can identify several problems. In what ways might I reduce the computational time to solve the model? In what ways might I maximize the amount of managerial information obtained from the model? In what ways can I get my solution accepted? In what ways can I develop a model useful for budgeting and planning? Or for detailed production scheduling? Viewed in this fashion, the modeling process is not as straightforward as you might believe.

Idea-finding

Idea-finding in model development often can be stimulated by graphic representations of the problem.[10] A graphic representation allows the modeler to see more easily the interrelationships among the various parts of the system being studied and therefore can generate ideas more easily. Simulation modeling makes extensive use of graphic descriptions. Shannon observes that

> the main purpose of the flow chart and/or block diagram is to aid in the analysis and communication of the logical structure of the system and the relationship of its elements. This is especially important during the definition of the system, since at that time we often do not know how the system should or does operate.[11]

Mathematical models are descriptions of systems; therefore, it is reasonable to use a graphic framework for representing them.[12] We shall represent the coffee bean problem as a graphic network: a collection of nodes representing physical objects, conceptual entities, or descriptors—and links, which connect the nodes. In the problem statement, we see that three blends of coffee are produced and two types of beans are used. Moreover, each bean can be used in each blend, and the beans have a limited availability. Furthermore, we see that production of the blends generates cost and that sales of the blends generate revenue; these contribute to profit. Figure 6–3 shows the general structure of the problem. On the links, we have provided numerical values that define relationships among the nodes.

The objective is to maximize profit. This graphic representation of the problem suggests several ways of defining variables. We do not know how

Figure 6–3 Structure of the Coffee Bean Problem

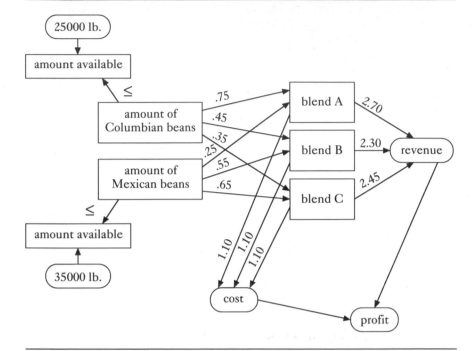

much of each blend to produce (associated with the nodes for each blend), how much of each bean to use in each blend (associated with the links between the bean nodes and the blend nodes), or the number of pounds of each type of bean to use (associated with the bean nodes). We might be able to model the problem using any one of these variable definitions or some *combination* of them. Four distinct models can easily be identified.

Model 1

x^A, x^B, x^C = number of lbs. of blends A, B, and C to produce
max $2.7x^A + 2.3x^B + 2.45x^C - 1.1(x^A + x^B + x^C)$
s.t. $.75x^A + .45x^B + .35x^C \le 25{,}000$
$.25x^A + .55x^B + .65x^C \le 35{,}000$
x^A, x^B, $x^C \ge 0$

Model 2

x_{CA} = number of lbs. of Colombians beans in blend A
x_{MA} = number of lbs. of Mexican beans in blend A
. . . and so on.
max $2.7 (x_{CA} + x_{MA}) + 2.3(x_{CB} + x_{MB}) + 2.45(x_{CC} + x_{MC})$

$$- 1.1\ (x_{CA} + x_{CB} + x_{CC} + x_{MA} + x_{MB} + x_{MC})$$
$$\text{s.t. } x_{CA} + x_{CB} + x_{CC} \leq 25{,}000$$
$$x_{MA} + x_{MB} + x_{MC} \leq 35{,}000$$
$$x_{CA} = .75(x_{CA} + x_{MA})$$
$$x_{CB} = .45(x_{CB} + x_{MB})$$
$$x_{CC} = .35(x_{CC} + x_{MC})$$
$$x_A, x_B, x_C \geq 0$$

Model 3

$x_A, x_B, x_C =$ number of lbs. of blends A, B, and C to produce
$x_1, x_2 =$ number of lbs. of Colombian and Mexican beans used, respectively

$$\max 2.7x_A + 2.3x_B + 2.45x_C - 1.1(x_1 + x_2)$$
$$\text{s.t. } .75x_A + .45x_B + .35x_C = x_1$$
$$.25x_A + .55x_B + .65x_C = x_2$$
$$x_1 \leq 25{,}000$$
$$x_2 \leq 35{,}000$$
$$x_A, x_B, x_C, x_1, x_2 \geq 0$$

Model 4
This model is a combination of models 1, 2, and 3.

$$\max 2.7x_A + 2.3x_B + 2.45x_C - 1.1(x_1 + x_2)$$
$$x_1 \leq 25{,}000$$
$$x_2 \leq 35{,}000$$
$$x_A = x_{CA} + x_{MA}$$
$$x_B = x_{CB} + x_{MB}$$
$$x_C = x_{CC} + x_{MC}$$
$$x_1 = x_{CA} + x_{CB} + x_{CC}$$
$$x_2 = x_{MA} + x_{MB} + x_{MC}$$
$$x_{CA} = .75x_A$$
$$x_{CB} = .45x_B$$
$$x_{CC} = .35x_C$$
$$x_A, x_B, x_C, x_1, x_2, x_{CA}, x_{CB}, x_{CC}, x_{MA}, x_{MB}, x_{MC} \geq 0$$

Solution-finding and Acceptance-finding

The solution-finding phase calls for evaluation and adoption of one of these models. If the model is to be used for budgeting or aggregate planning, then model 1 may suffice, since it provides the total profit and the production of the final products. If the model is to be used for detailed production scheduling, then model 2 may be more appropriate, since it provides a detailed plan for blending that model 1 does not provide. If management is interested in detailed sensitivity analysis information, then model 4 may be the best, since all variables are explicitly represented.[13]

Application of the CPS Process to Model Solution: A Goal Programming Example

Consider the following problem.[14] A small paint company manufactures two types of paint, latex and oil-based. Each 100 gallons of latex requires 10 hours of labor and generates \$100 profit. A 100-gallon batch of oil-based paint requires 15 hours of labor and generates \$100 profit. Forty hours of labor are available, and the owner has set a goal of \$1,000 profit and has agreed to supply 700 gallons of oil-based paint to a friend if possible. Raw material limitations prohibit more than 800 gallons of latex and 500 gallons of oil-based paint from being made. The owner's goals are, first, to avoid overtime; second, to achieve the profit goal; and third, to supply his friend.

Letting x_1 = number of gallons of latex and x_2 = number of gallons of oil-based paint to produce, we have the following constraints:

$$10x_1 + 15x_2 + n_1 - p_1 = 40$$
$$100x_1 + 100x_2 + n_2 - p_2 = 1000$$
$$x_2 + n_3 - p_3 = 7$$

$$0 \le x_1 \le 8$$
$$0 \le x_2 \le 5$$
$$n_i, p_i \ge 0$$

where n_i and p_i are the deviations from the respective goals. One approach to goal programming is to treat the objective function as a weighted linear combination of the deviations. Thus, the objective function is

$$\text{minimize } k_1 p_1 + k_2 n_2 + k_3 n_3$$

where $k_1 < k_2 < k_3$ represent the relative weights, or priorities, associated with the three goals. The model is the "mess" that is to be solved. Let us consider the other steps of the CPS process.

Fact-finding

The obvious fact is that we have a linear goal program to solve. However, we may have limited software availability and limited time available to arrive at a solution. The time factor is not uncommon in real business situations when the boss wants an answer *tomorrow*! Other relevant facts might be the availability of a micro or mainframe computer.

Problem-finding

Does the decision maker simply want an answer or does he or she want to examine various scenarios in a "what if" context? For example, the decision maker may simply wish to evaluate a trial solution (perhaps the current operating environment), examine how well goals are being met, and then examine the effects of changes in a parameter or goal weight. Some problem perspectives might be: In what ways might I solve this model? In what ways might I use the model to examine various alternatives? In what ways might I solve this model if nonlinearities in the formulation are discovered?

Idea-finding

One obvious way to solve this model is to use a simplex method-based algorithm. Another is to use a special goal programming code, if available. A third approach, which is probably not obvious, is to use a **nonlinear** formulation of the model (**adapting** a technique from a different area, to place this in the context of Osborn's checklist). This can be done as follows. Let us examine the first constraint. If x_1 and x_2 are specified, then n_1 and p_1 are uniquely determined by the following:

$$n_1 = \max\{0, 40 - 10x_1 - 15x_2\}$$
$$p_1 = \max\{0, 10x_1 + 15x_2 - 40\}$$

The complete problem can be expressed as:

minimize $k_1 \max\{0, 10x_1 + 15x_2 - 40\} +$
$k_2 \max\{0, 1000 - 100x_1 - 100x_2\}$
$+ k_3 \max\{0, 7 - x_2\}$

subject to

$$0 \le x_1 \le 8$$
$$0 \le x_2 \le 5$$

Solution-finding and Acceptance-finding

What are the advantages of solving this model using the nonlinear formulation presented in the last section? First, one has not lost the ability to optimize. In fact, it is extremely easy to program an optimization code using an ordinary programming language. If nonlinearities arise in a revised model, this approach can handle them. The decision maker can easily investigate scenarios by simply inputting values for the decision variables and letting the program evaluate the goal attainments. A decision maker can "look" at a solution and decide on its merits relative to the formal goals *as well* as intangibles that cannot be captured in the model.

Postscript

This creative approach of using a nonlinear technique to solve a linear program of this type was proposed by Bruce Schmeiser some time ago.[15] The model was, of course, much larger, and nonlinearities did, in fact, arise after the initial model was proposed. The motivation for this approach was the fact that in the early 1970s, computer codes for LP and GP were expensive, not widely available, and not portable. The client was under time pressure to solve the problem and needed an answer quickly. The approach provided another distinct advantage in that the solution algorithm (a cyclic coordinate method) was easily explained, and the client understood and accepted the solution.

In this section we have presented three examples of how the Osborn/ Parnes creative problem-solving process can be applied in individual steps of the traditional operations research modeling methodology. While it certainly takes more effort to apply this process consciously, the benefits in the quality of the resulting solution can be substantial.

A CREATIVE ATMOSPHERE FOR MODELING

In the decision and management sciences, education is often criticized for containing too much theory and technique. More stress on problem definition and model-building skills has been suggested.[16] Stephen Pollock first recognized that while practitioners agree that mathematical modeling is an art and rather difficult to teach, practicing "creative" artists (for example, painters, sculptors, and musicians) seem to have little problem in teaching the skills of their art to students.[17] However, their teaching is rarely done in a formal classroom setting, but rather in an artist's studio. Working from this analogy, he proposed "The Modeling Studio," which should have the following attributes:

1. Encouragement of excess. The visual arts encourage excess in order for the student to discover his or her own limitations and that of the medium. In DS/MS, one can also "push" a model to its limits by relaxing deterministic assumptions or changing linear functions to nonlinear ones, for example. All of the creativity stimulants that we have discussed in this book can be applied. However, Pollock emphasizes that excess is not recommended in actual modeling, but rather in learning *how* to model. Clearly, the focus should be on developing creativity and the facility for idea generation.
2. Philosophy: "post," not "pre." Discussing the philosophy of modeling should occur *after* the details are developed, not before. Early

discussion of philosophy might tend to create functional fixations and discourage creative discovery.

3. Data. The inclusion of data (and dirty data) is important to provide a realistic environment.

4. No data. This helps to create a tolerance for ambiguity. The inclusion of data can lead to unwarranted conclusions or generalizations.

5. The availability of experts who do not know everything. Experts do not always have the most creative solutions. How many "experts" would think of solving a goal program using a nonlinear optimization algorithm as shown in the previous section?

6. Skepticism of others. There is no "model" model. Recall that skepticism is one of the fundamental traits of creative individuals.

7. Criticism of self. Students should be able to point out weak points in analysis.

8. A foundation, but not "pilings," of techniques. This suggests that one learn not only mathematical tools, but also social psychology, organizational structure, and other areas where classical models exist: physics, chemistry, psychology, economics, and so on. Avoid "pilings" (that is, a math programmer who has "pilings" of linear programming, nonlinear programming, dynamic programming, and network theory should not be expected to describe population growth processes well). This clearly suggests the need for expanding knowledge into broader fields of study.

Such attributes are clearly among those that are conducive to a creative climate as proposed by creative-thinking writers. A course in problem solving should provide students with the following:[18]

1. basic technical, manipulative, and computing skills
2. attitude and will to solve problems and tackle new situations, not just categorize them
3. ability to obtain information
4. communication skills
5. ability to work in groups
6. experiences from which to make judgments
7. understanding of how the students have solved problems

Students must be able to take a problem apart, generalize, be creative, generate hypotheses, do mathematics, draw logical inferences, and make decisions. Some suggestions for the professor: have students work problems on the board and describe how they did it; change the learning environment, perhaps by using a game; or prepare problems for the professor, who would think out loud while solving them.

Many new teaching tools in DS/MS have been proposed in recent years:

1. the use of short cases[19]
2. street experience and field consultation[20]

3. the use of computer software for realistic applications[21]
4. the integration of creative-thinking principles in case problem solving[22]
5. actually doing what the "worker bees" are doing in the present system to gain knowledge and credibility[23]

McPherson listed a set of questions that organizations interested in creativity should address. These are listed here as concluding remarks and food for thought for decision science educators and practitioners:[24]

> Do we select people capable of the dedication that unique problem solving and creative solutions require? Do we reward them properly to maintain their motivation? Do we have a balance between expecting unique solutions from the range of time demands (today's operations, tomorrow's expectations, and the future)? Do we have a greater number of people aware of the wide range of problem solving methods available and skill in using them? Does our system provide individuals with satisfactory feedback about their personal performance and the fate of their ideas? Are we one of the many constraints in our system that legislate against the creativity of our people? Are managers prepared to accept multiple efforts that will be exerted upon them if they have a highly creative population?

In the future, problem solving will depend on creative solutions. The decision and management sciences have a unique opportunity for training individuals in these skills, and we must take advantage of this challenge.

EXERCISES

1. Find and read some good applied papers in *Interfaces*, such as the Franz Edelman award winners, and describe the problem-solving process, using both the classical OR framework and the Parnes/Osborn creative problem-solving process. What are the differences? Can you point to any specific advantages of one over the other?

2. Select textbook problem statements like the linear programming example in the text. Illustrate how the creative problem-solving process can be applied to develop a model.

3. Various case books in DS/MS exist.[25] Apply the creative problem-solving process to the solution of an unstructured case problem.

4. Discuss other ways in which the various creativity-enhancement tools of Chapter 4 can be used in modeling and algorithm development in DS/MS.

ENDNOTES

1. Arthur B. VanGundy, "Comparing 'Little Known' Creative Problem Solving Techniques," in *Creativity Week III, 1980 Proceedings* (Greensboro, NC: Center for Creative Leadership, 1981).

2. C. West Churchman, Russell L. Ackoff, and E. Leonard Arnoff, *Introduction to Operations Research* (New York: John Wiley & Sons, 1957).

3. Harvey J. Brightman, *Problem Solving: A Logical and Creative Approach* (Atlanta, GA: Business Publishing Division, College of Business Administration, Georgia State University, 1980).

4. This illustration is adapted from a consulting assignment with which the author was involved.

5. Gerhard Knolmayer, "Computational Experiments in the Formulation of Linear Product-Mix and Non-Convex Production-Investment Models," *Computers and Operations Research* 9, no. 3 (1982): pp. 207–19.

6. John D.C. Little, "Models and Managers: The Concept of a Decision Calculus," *Management Science* 16, no. 8 (1970): pp. B466–85.

7. William T. Morris, "On the Art of Modeling," *Management Science* 13, no. 12 (1967): pp. B707–17. This paper is highly recommended to all readers and remains a classic in the field.

8. Woolsey's Law of Acceptability: Acceptability = 1/Complexity.

9. David R. Anderson, Dennis J. Sweeney, and Thomas A. Williams, *Introduction to Management Science, 5th ed.* (St. Paul, MN: West Publishing, 1987).

10. Formal graphical approaches to modeling include influence diagrams (which arose in the context of decision analysis) and artificial intelligence tools such as semantic networks. Patrick Rivett's book, *Principles of Model Building* (London: John Wiley & Sons, 1972), provides similar diagrammatic methods for expressing model relationships.

11. Robert E. Shannon, *Systems Simulation: The Art and Science* (Englewood Cliffs, NJ: Prentice-Hall, 1975).

12. J.R. Evans and J.D. Camm, "Using Pictorial Representations in Teaching Linear Programming Modeling," *IIE Transactions* 22 (1990): pp. 191–95.

13. An excellent discussion of the issues of linear programming modeling and sensitivity analysis can be found in Leonard W. Swanson, *Linear Programming, Basic Theory and Applications* (New York: McGraw-Hill, 1980). Jeffrey D. Camm, P.M. Dearing, and Suresh K. Tadisina, "The Calhoun Textile Mill Case: An Exercise on the Significance of Linear Programming Model Formulation," *IIE Transactions* 19, no. 1: pp. 23–28, also provides a case study on this issue.

14. Adapted from James Ignizio, *Goal Programming and Extensions* (Lexington, MA: Lexington Press, 1976).

15.   Bruce W. Schmeiser, "Some Practical Reasons for Using Nonlinear Techniques in Certain Linear Programming Applications," presented at the ORSA/TIMS National Meeting, Chicago, 1975.

16.   H. Brightman and C. Noble, "On the Ineffective Education of Decision Scientists," *Decision Sciences* 10 (1979) pp. 151–57, and R.H McClure, "Educating the Future Users of O.R.," *Interfaces* 11, no. 5 (1981) pp. 108–12.

17.   Stephen M. Pollock, "The Modeling Studio (Discouraging the Model Model)," presented at the ORSA/TIMS National Meeting, Boston, 1974. This concept was extended by Michael Magazine in "The Problem Solving Studio," (Waterloo, Ontario, Canada: Department of Management Sciences, University of Waterloo).

18.   Based on D. Woods, "On Teaching Problem Solving—Parts I and II," *Chemical Engineering Education* 21 (Spring and Summer 1987): pp. 86–94 and 140–44.

19.   R. Aggarwal and I. Khera, "Short Cases for Teaching Management Science: Their Role in Closing the Gap Between Theory and Practice," *Interfaces* 90, no. 6 (1978): pp. 90–94. See also M.J.C. Martin, "Short Cases for Teaching Management Science: An Extended Comment," *Interfaces* 10, no. 2 (1980): pp. 10–12.

20.   W.C. Giauque, "Taking the Classroom Into Reality: A Field Consulting Experience for MBAs," *Interfaces* 10, no. 4 (1980): pp. 1–10; L.F. Gelders, "Introducing Field Consulting in the Industrial Management Curriculum," *Interfaces* 11, no. 2 (1981): pp. 1–7; and W.C. Giauque and R.E.D. Woolsey, "A Totally New Direction for Management Education: A Modest Proposal," *Interfaces* 11, no. 4 (1981): pp. 30–34.

21.   B. Render and R.M. Stair, Jr., "The Use of Computer Programs in Management Science Eduction," *Interfaces* 11, no. 3 (1981): pp. 75–79.

22.   James R. Evans, "Creative Thinking and Innovative Education in the Decision Sciences," *Decision Sciences* 17, no. 2 (1986): pp. 250–62.

23.   Gene Woolsey, private communication.

24.   J.H. McPherson, "The People, The Problems, and The Problem Solving Methods," in S.J. Parnes, R.B. Noeller, and A.M. Biondi, eds., *Guide to Creative Action* (New York: Scribners, 1977).

25.   R. Aggarwal and I. Khera, *Management Science: Cases and Applications* (San Francisco: Holden-Day, 1979); M.J.C. Martin and R.A. Denison, *Case Exercises in Operations Research* (Wiley-Interscience, 1971); E.F. Peter Newson, ed., *Management Science and the Manager: A Casebook* (Englewood Cliffs, NJ: Prentice-Hall, 1980); and B. Render, R.M. Stair, and I. Greenberg, *Cases and Readings in Management Science 2d ed.* (Boston: Allyn & Bacon, 1990).

CHAPTER 7
Creative Thinking and Research in the Decision and Management Sciences

INTRODUCTION

Research is fundamental to the growth of any scientific discipline. In comparison with other well-established fields of science such as mathematics, chemistry, or psychology, the decision and management sciences are in their infancy. Research, in both academia and in industry, is necessary to advance the field and to solve the new and increasingly complex problems that continually arise. Since research is highly unstructured, creativity is vitally important to its success. In this chapter we focus on elements of creativity and the creative problem-solving process in research.

This chapter is directed primarily toward graduate students and professors who wish to develop better skills in performing research, especially in identifying research problems. However, it is not restricted to this audience. This material also would be helpful to practitioners involved in corporate consulting and research-related activities. We begin this chapter with a discussion of research and the research process from a general perspective.

PERSPECTIVES ON RESEARCH

Webster's *Third New International Dictionary* defines *research* as "critical and exhaustive investigation or experimentation having for its aim the discovery of new facts and their correct interpretation, the revision of accepted conclusions, theories, or laws in the light of newly discovered facts, or the practical application of such new or revised conclusions, theories, or laws" (p. 1930). A more applied definition is given by Emory:[1] Research is "any organized inquiry carried out to provide information for solving problems (including) descriptive, predictive, and explanatory studies." Thus, research in scientific fields is carried out to describe, explain, and predict.

Research generally is partitioned into two categories: **basic** and **applied**. Basic research (also called **pure** or **fundamental** research) is focused on establishing or discovering new scientific facts without regard to specific applications or commerical use. We conduct basic research to improve our understanding of phenomena and to add to the existing body of knowledge in a discipline. Applied research is focused on the continual improvement of new goods and services and on solving specific problems experienced by an organization. Universities are primarily engaged in basic research, while industry is chiefly focused on applied research. However, it is not unusual to find these roles reversed.

Basic research typically follows the **scientific method**. The scientific method is a systematic process in which a problem is identified, data is collected and analyzed, and valid conclusions are drawn from the analysis. The scientific method is characterized by several important attributes. The research must be **critical, analytical, and logical**; that is, based on a formal process using rigorous tools and methods that lead to analytical conclusions. Research must be **objective** so that it can be replicated by others. It is not based on hunches or intuition alone, and it is grounded in sound methodological design. **Theoretical** knowledge is used to guide the research efforts, while **empirical** study is needed to anchor the research to reality.

For example, the research objectives of the National Science Foundation's program in the Decision and Management Sciences (DMS) emphasize the creation of a theoretical and empirical science of managerial and operational processes.[2] The DMS mission statement characterizes this research in the following manner:

> In the conduct of research, processes will typically be characterized by mathematical, logical, and statistical models. These models will be derived from empirical observation, or from theory that is subject to empirical verification. Empirical analyses should be pursued in some operational context, but the emphasis should be on theories, findings and methods that are generalizable to other contexts.
>
> Thus, the body of research supported by the program should possess *generality*, be based on *empirical* observation or be subject to empirical validation, and incorporate *social and behavioral* aspects. Processes should be characterized by *models* that are tested in *operational contexts*. Even though an individual project may not have all these characteristics, its evolution toward this end must be clear.

Applied research in industry began in 1902 when Du Pont's first formal research laboratory was started.[3] In 1920 about 300 research laboratories were functioning; and in 1950, over 2,800. Today, nearly every major corporation has research laboratories for new product development.

In addition to product research, supporting services such as internal management-science consulting groups conduct applied research in solving operational problems. Evidence of the success of management-science research in industry can be found in the annual Franz Edelman International Prize Competition sponsored by The Institute of Management Sciences and its College on the Practice of Management Science. The awards were established in 1972 to recognize and honor outstanding examples of implemented management-science projects. The prize is awarded to the client organization in recognition of its use of high-impact management science. Franz Edelman was responsible for one of the earliest industrial management-science activities at RCA. He was also a pioneering advocate of computers for the analysis of business problems throughout industry. The papers prepared by the finalists in each year's competition are published in *Interfaces*. You are strongly encouraged to read and study these articles for many examples of the creative use of management science.

The Research Process[4]

The process of conducting research is described in Figure 7-1. This process applies equally to basic and applied research. The need for a research study begins with an awareness of a broad problem area that requires research. Preliminary data gathering, either through observation or literature review, is

Figure 7-1 The Research Process

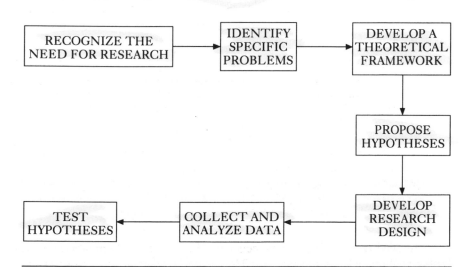

conducted. Next, the specific research problems are identified. A theoretical framework, or conceptual model of how important factors are related, is developed. This provides a scientific basis for the research problem. To test whether or not the relationships among important variables that have been theorized are true, hypotheses are developed. Hypotheses are logically conjectured relationships between two or more variables; they are expressed in the form of testable statements. The research design specifies the purpose of the study, type of investigation, limitations, data collection procedures, methods of measurement, and methods of analysis. We then collect and analyze data, and accept or reject hypotheses through deduction. Deduction is the process of drawing inferences through logical analysis. It is important to realize that this process is not linear but cyclic in nature. Often we must return to prior steps as new information becomes available.

Types of Research

Meredith et al. suggest that research involves a continuous, repetitive cycle of description, explanation, and testing (through prediction). Proposing knowledge (explanation) and validating knowledge (testing) are simply two stages in the cycle of research.[5]

Descriptive research seeks to report and chronicle elements of situations and events to improve understanding of the subject of interest. This characterization may be used to generate hypotheses that can be formally tested. Hypothesis generation often results from exploratory research in which a particular aspect is investigated in more detail.

Explanatory research consists of postulating hypotheses about a situation. These may be some type of cause-and-effect relationship or a more complex set of relationships—a framework—that explains the interrelationships. Frameworks help researchers design specific research studies, interpret existing research, and generate testable hypotheses. When a framework is shown to describe the principles operating in a situation, it is often called a theory. A theory is a set of general principles that explains observed facts, but it also must include the interrelationships among its variables and/or attributes, as well as some criteria that define its boundaries. The theory must also improve our understanding of the non-unique phenomenon or help us make predictions about it.[6]

Testing is performed to determine which hypotheses are correct and which are false, and how to modify or expand them. The process commonly involves a prediction based on the explanation constructed and then observation to determine if the prediction was correct. Alternatively, a prediction may be proposed and then checked against observations already made or included in the description. This stage uses rigorous statistical tools or experimentation, often leading to more description or exploratory investigation.

Research can begin at various stages of this cycle. Research can be deductive, in which theoretical models are developed that lead to empirical observation and testing; or it can be inductive, in which empirical observation leads to the development of theories.

THE ROLE OF CREATIVITY IN RESEARCH

Earlier in this book we noted that three important elements of creativity are knowledge, imagination, and evaluation. In science and engineering, knowledge is vital, since the scientist or engineer must master an enormous body of knowledge before he or she can attempt to do serious research. Having this knowledge, however, is the first step toward creative research. As in the kaleidoscope analogy, knowledge provides more ways in which to be creative.

It has been suggested that the accumulation of knowledge in a discipline follows one of two epistemologies.[7] One approach describes knowledge accumulation as if many researchers were throwing mud at a wall. The mud that sticks to the wall (i.e., is published, or more appropriately, is *used*) is knowledge and should be retained. That which falls off should be discarded. This viewpoint suggests that the more individuals there are throwing different kinds of mud, the more likely it is that some of them will throw something that sticks. While this viewpoint corresponds to the creativity principle that quantity breeds quality, many criticize it as breeding a large amount of poor research; burdening journal editors, reviewers, and conference programmers; and making truly significant research more difficult. Many point the finger of blame at the publish-or-perish tenure system in our universities as a prime contributor to these problems.

A second viewpoint suggests that knowledge accumulates from individuals carefully mapping out areas likely to yield good information and results, rather than from randomly searching. This approach avoids duplication, provides better insight, eliminates old mistakes, and builds creatively on past findings.

We suggest that the creative problem-solving process can be applied to the research process and specifically to the identification of research problems, thus improving the quality of both activities. Knowledge beyond one's own immediate field is important for creativity. Saaty observes that the inclination toward independent thought can easily be stunted by overspecialization. One's talents are frequently so thoroughly absorbed in techniques that little opportunity remains for the broader creative abilities one might possess.[8] He quotes Bernard Koopman as stating that "a specialist who works all his life in one field may produce a great succession of papers. But too often it happens that a sameness of thought sets in, and every result looks like every other; the morning light is lost. A little of the spirit of the amateur may give much of the spirit of adventure and is . . . closer to the freshness in the air of discovery."[9] When one changes one's field of study, not only is there the "freshness" of new ideas, but a much greater opportunity to apply one's former knowledge and experience in new ways.

Osborn observes that imagination supplies the springboard for knowledge. The path to any research project must be paved with ideas. Imagination is the essence of research; it enables us to look beyond existing knowledge to wonder what can be; to experiment; and to form hypotheses that can be verified, thus adding to existing knowledge. A research idea is a creative product. We cannot produce one on demand; it typically arise from unconscious thought. But, as we have seen in this book, we can consciously foster the production of ideas.

Finally, evaluation is crucial in determining if our research results are useful and how they impact the discipline, either by enhancing basic knowledge or providing means of solving problems that were previously difficult or impossible to solve.

Experimentation is the foundation for evaluation. Creative research is full of questions such as, What if? How about? What else? Is it true? Will it work? Creativity is important, since there are many ways in which experiments may be designed and conducted. New concepts arise from experiments and observations, and these lead to further experiments and observations.

Characteristics of Researchers

Creativity demands greater flexibility in science and engineering than in almost any other occupation. The scientist must master an enormous body of knowledge that is changing rapidly. Yet the researcher also must be as imaginative as an artist or musician. He or she also must have the ability to relate ideas to reality, to test their validity, and to develop them further.[10]

Research is a creative process consisting of divergent and convergent activities. Divergent activities include observing facts without judgment or premature evaluation and generating hypotheses. Convergent activities involve testing and confirming or rejecting these hypotheses. Research demands not only flexibility and imagination, but also well-organized thought processes and logic. These characteristics often are the opposite of creative characteristics; this might explain why many individuals in technical areas find it difficult to be creative.

Several studies have shown that scientists and engineers are most creative in the "thirtysomething" years.[11] This typically is the first decade out of graduate school, after several years of total immersion in acquiring deep knowledge in a subject area. This pattern is also true for practitioners. As career responsibilities change, however, research productivity dwindles. For example, a tenured professor might devote more time to service rather than research, or a business analyst might assume increased managerial responsibilities.

An interesting study by Hitt and Stock investigated the characteristics of researchers in terms of originality and logical reasoning.[12] Drawing from prior research, they classified researchers into four categories:

Type I: high originality, high logical reasoning
Type II: high originality, low logical reasoning
Type III: low originality, low logical reasoning
Type IV: low originality, high logical reasoning

Hitt and Stock studied a group of 96 scientists and engineers in a research lab, 24 in each group, selected from 200 researchers.

The results from this study are summarized as follows. The type I researcher is found to be above the sample average in general intelligence and to do well in both divergent and convergent thinking. He or she is an original thinker, not cautious, able to identify problems, responsible and energetic. The Type II researcher is good at divergent thinking and views himself or herself as an original thinker, not cautious, enjoys mixing with people, assertive in a group, and can generate a large number of ideas. The Type III researcher is below the average in general intelligence, cautious, trusts others, and is not self-assertive. Finally, the Type IV researcher is very responsible, emotionally stable, and tends to be cautious. He or she is about equal to Type II in general intelligence but does not do well in divergent thinking and does not assert himself/herself in group situations.

This study has several implications for researchers in DS/MS. Since creativity requires both convergent and divergent thinking, both logical reasoning and originality are necessary. Most DS/MS analysts are very good at logical reasoning and therefore are good at convergent thinking. This includes mathematical proofs, algorithm development, and so forth. However, most need help in divergent thinking; that is, the identification of problems and the generation of ideas. My experience has been that graduate students are quite good at doing research if the problems are given to them; they are generally poor at identifying their own problems. Similar statements hold for analysts in business.

THE CREATIVE PROBLEM-SOLVING PROCESS IN RESEARCH

As we have seen in Chapter 6, the Osborn/Parnes creative problem-solving process can play a useful role in enhancing traditional operations-research methodology. In this section we discuss its usefulness in the research process.

Let us assume the role of a graduate student who is seeking a thesis or dissertation topic. He or she certainly faces a **mess**: In what general topic area should I focus my attention to research? Mess-finding, then, involves a broad understanding of the various subfields of the discipline to determine the area in which one's interests and strengths lie. Certainly one must acquire a broad exposure to the field through different courses. Which topics are already well researched? Which pose new and exciting opportunities?

One must also do some serious introspection. For example, an operations research student must ask: Am I more comfortable with deterministic models or stochastic models? If my preference is deterministic models, for instance, am I intrigued by integer programming, multicriteria optimization, nonlinear algorithms, or networks? An operations management student might consider whether he or she works best with analytical models or with empirical investigation and analysis. Any student should ask, why? Why do I need a Ph.D.? Answers to such questions are needed to resolve the mess and select a general area of interest.

The second phase of the process is fact-finding. This is normally accomplished by a thorough literature review. Nationally known experts often publish position papers about the "hot" topics in a particular discipline.[13] Opportunities for significant research are often found by classifying relevant literature in an area. For example, Richard Chase developed a classification scheme for operations management research along two dimensions of research orientation (macro or micro) and research emphasis (people or equipment), as shown in Figure 7-2.[14] His analysis of papers in the late 1970s showed that the vast majority fell into the micro-equipment quadrant, while no papers were published in the macro-people quadrant. This clearly showed a gap in the research literature that could result in significant research.

An excellent example of a detailed literature review and classification scheme that is useful for identifying research problems is given in a paper by Bahl, Ritzman, and Gupta.[15] They investigate production planning lot-sizing problems and classify them into four categories: single level (independent demand) with unconstrained resources (SLUR); single level with constrained resources (SLCR); multiple level (dependent demand) with unconstrained resources (MLUR); and multiple level with constrained resources (MLCR). The literature review should not only summarize the important research concerning a selected topic, but it should also critically evaluate the strengths and weaknesses of existing results. Figure 7-3 shows an example of an evaluation of selected research on the SLCR problem. Such an analysis often provides good ideas for potential research topics by noting missing "gaps" in the literature. For instance, Bahl et al. suggest that one might

    a.   develop ways to enrich the single-resource heuristics that assume setups without any loss of capacity, perhaps through some type of iterative solution procedure;

    b.   identify the manufacturing environments in which the departure from optimality is greatest when applying the less general heuristics;

    c.   intensify efforts to test existing and new heuristics for the quality

Figure 7-2 Classification Scheme for Operations Management

RESEARCH ORIENTATION

		MICRO	MACRO
R E S E A R C H E M P H A S I S	P E O P L E	Work measurement [1]	
	E Q U I P M E N T	2 | 1	
		3 | 4	
		Inventory control [2] Scheduling [1] Facility layout Process design Maintenance & reliability [2] Quality control Capacity planning Aggregate planning	Facility location [3]

[ ] denotes secondary quadrant

and of their solutions and the efficiency of their computation—and to ascertain whether some have a comparative advantage in certain manufacturing environments.

Problem-finding in research can be viewed as selecting a specific research problem to investigate. A research study should fill some important void in current knowledge. While a literature review may provide many suggestions of problems to investigate, the researcher must ask some fundamental questions (Can I get the answer? Will it help? How much will it cost? What is the payoff? Is everyone else doing it?) and most important, Am I interested?[16]

Idea-finding and solution-finding involve the analysis and selection of an appropriate research methodology for addressing the problem. Meredith et al. provide a comprehensive review of alternative research methodologies in operations management.[17] Examples of research methodologies would include normative and descriptive modeling, simulation, surveys, case and field studies, action research, expert panels, and scenario analysis. The use of different methodologies can provide unique perspectives on the research question being investigated. One should consider the use of nontraditional methodologies during this phase of the process.

Figure 7-3 Example of Literature Review and Evaluation (from Bahl et al.)

Description of Work	Selected Research on SLCR Problem						
	Classification Criteria[a]					Strength	Weakness
	C	G	O	S	T		
Manne (1958): Lot sizing with resource constraints	Poor	Good	No	Fair	Poor	Novel problem formulation amenable to linear programming	Large number of variables; nonoptimal solution
Dzielinski, Baker and Manne (1963): Simulation tests of using EOQ vs. Manne's model	N/A	N/A	N/A	N/A	N/A	Tests Manne's approach	Tested with only one real-life problem
Dzielinski and Gomory (1965): Applies Dantzig-Wolfe Decomposition to Manne's model	Fair	Good	No	Poor	Fair	Larger problems are amenable to solution	Lack simplicity in understanding
Lasdon and Terjung (1967): Applies Column Generation method to Manne's model	Good	Good	No	Poor	Fair	Computational efficiency over earlier approaches; better bounds on solution	Lacks simplicity in understanding
Newson (1975): Heuristic method for lot-sizing problem	Good	Fair	No	Fair	Fair	Computational savings	Not tested for multiple work centers
Haessler (1979): Simple heuristic for ELSP	Good	Poor	No	Good	Poor	Simple and efficient	Assumes constant demand and single resource

Selected Research on SLCR Problem

Description of Work	Classification Criteria[a]					Strength	Weakness
	C	G	O	S	T		
Dixon and Silver (1981): Single-resource heuristic	Good	Poor	No	Good	Good	Very good solutions with little computational effort	Single resource; setup times assumed negligible
Aras and Swanson (1982): Single-resource heuristic to expanded problem	Good	Good	No	Good	Fair	Incorporates sequencing decisions; setup times apply to capacity constraints	Single resource and limited testing
Bahl and Ritzman (1983): Heuristic method for Manne's formulation	Good	Good	No	Good	Fair	Additional computational savings	Limited testing
Bahl (1983): Heuristic method for Manne's formulation	Good	Good	No	Poor	Fair	Efficiency gains over column generation	Limited testing
Daniels (1983): Multiple-resource heuristic to expanded problem	Good	Good	No	Fair	Fair	Incorporates sequencing decisions; sequence-dependent setups are part of capacity constraints; multiple resources	Heuristic method, and lacks transparency in understanding

[a] C = computational effort, compared to other SLCR procedures, G = generality to all SLCR problems, O = optimality, S = simplicity in understanding, T = thorough testing, if heuristic.

Finally, acceptance-finding involves assessing the potential benefits of the research, and of course, whether or not it might be accepted by a journal or a thesis committee!

RESEARCH STRATEGIES IN THE DECISION AND MANAGEMENT SCIENCES

Studies of published literature in DS/MS reveal several major categories of research and provide a useful classification scheme as well as a better understanding of how to generate research ideas.[18] Many of these strategies can be enhanced through common creativity stimulants that are discussed in Chapter 3.

Incremental Improvements

This strategy involves incremental improvements to existing work. Some examples of types of incremental research are listed below.

1. Limitations or strong points of existing results. This is mainly descriptive research aimed at further understanding of existing theories or techniques through critical evaluation.
2. Modification of known results and procedures. Examples include computational improvements in algorithms, the use of heuristics in place of an exact algorithm, or the development of special algorithms for special cases of a general problem.
3. Variations on existing problems. This might involve changing assumptions or restrictions on a problem, or studying a problem with a new optimality criterion.

The incremental improvement strategy is probably the most common academic approach to research. It is a safe and comfortable way to go, and it is rather easy to identify new research questions. However, it is difficult to gain a significant breakthrough by using this strategy. Significant breakthroughs require an extension of a well-developed body of theory; this is very difficult to do. Incremental improvement also demands high technical competence in a specific area and is best suited "for those with great skills for analysis but who lack the additional creativity needed to do synthesis or design."

Generalization

This strategy represents the case in which several known models or theories are embedded into a more generalized formulation or a global theory.

This is the "big leap forward." Such research is primarily theoretical, based on logical deduction of previously published works. It does not require computerization or data. However, it does require the most creativity and can result in more significant contributions.

Merging Ideas

Merging known models or theories is a common research strategy. An example would be the merging of computer science data structures with network optimization algorithms that occurred in the 1970s. This strategy does not require great creativity but does require technical versatility as well as competence. The researcher must understand each of the disciplines that he or she is working in and must be knowledgeable and convinced that bridging is necessary.

Knowledge Transfer

This strategy uses what is known in one discipline to model problem domains falling in another discipline—for instance, the use of network flow models for cash management. It is often based on analogies, which, as we have seen, are an important component of creative thinking. Simulated annealing is a prime example of such an approach. The concept of annealing in thermodynamics was adapted directly to problems in combinatorial optimization.

Creative Application Strategy

In this approach, one applies directly, not by analogy, a known methodology to a problem not previously so addressed. An example is the use of mathematical programming to jet engine maintenance and repair.[19] Today, it is becoming more and more difficult to find areas that have *not* been addressed by DS/MS. However, this points out the need to broaden your scope of knowledge into different areas to develop creative applications.

Emerging Disciplines

Related to the creative application strategy is the notion of identifying a set of problems that have been unexplored by management-science techniques. For example, operations researchers discovered applications in criminal justice in the 1960s. More recently, we have seen a plethora of papers dealing with operations research models in computer networks and information systems; the service sector quickly is becoming an important area of operations management research. As Reisman states, such a strategy is usually a "publishing bonanza," with many new papers being written in these areas.

Empirical Research

Empirical research in DS/MS is generally of two types. The first involves validating a general theory through empirical research. Many models in the social sciences dealing with organizational behavior or implementation processes are first developed as theoretical constructs that require empirical validation. A second type of empirical research is the comparison of different solution techniques for a class of problems to determine which is better or under what conditions one method is better than another (predictive research). In the latter case, one generates a knowledge base similar to that in an expert system. For example, if conditions x, y, and z hold, then algorithm 1 is better. On the other hand, if conditions x and w are true, then algorithm 2 is better. Empirical research is often labor- and computer-intensive, requiring the design of a data-collection instrument, or the generation of test problems, and the collection and analysis of data. It requires the least creativity and breadth of vision, since it simply involves experimental work on prior results.

IDENTIFYING GOOD
RESEARCH PROBLEMS

Psychologists really do not know how individuals generate good research questions. Like any creative idea, the accumulation of knowledge, persistence, incubation, and inspiration seem to describe the process. However, as we have seen throughout this book, we can facilitate idea generation through conscious application of creative-thinking concepts.

First, let us demonstrate how the CPS process provides structured guidelines for identifying research problems. The mess is the result of the literature-review phase. One has a messy collection of facts, theories, empirical and/or theoretical results about a particular problem. The fact-finding phase can be approached best through some method of classification, as discussed using the example by Bahl et al. Problem-finding is the determination of "gaps" in the knowledge. Idea-finding is the generation of potential hypotheses that can fill these gaps. Solution-finding involves determining a hypothesis or set of hypotheses that promises to advance knowledge. Finally, acceptance-finding involves justification of the research question.

In selecting a research problem, the researcher must be capable of solving it, given the tools and knowledge available—or at least the solution must stand a remote chance of being found. Not all research studies are successful, and the researcher must be prepared for numerous failures. Remember that persistence is crucial to creativity. Long, intensive, persistent effort almost always precedes a major scientific discovery. The problem should also represent a creative breakthrough. Often the creative implications are obvious if one can solve a particular problem. In other cases the researcher does not see the possibility of a creative discovery at the beginning but pursues the idea simply because it is intriguing.

A study by Campbell, Daft, and Hulin in the organizational behavior area provided some insights into why "good" versus "poor" research ideas are identified.[20] Their study involved a convenience sample of 29 scholars, a questionnaire, and semistructured interviews. Successful and significant research was found to result from the following:

1. Activity. Successful researchers frequently interacted with colleagues, and these interactions often spawned good research ideas. Researchers who worked in isolation were less likely to generate significant research.
2. Convergence. Several activities or interests seemed to converge at the same time—for example, the combination of an idea with a method or the mutual interest of a professor with a student. This is related to activity as the researcher is able to use different streams of investigation.
3. Intuition. The importance of the research seems to be guided by intuition rather than by logical analysis. Investigators often expressed a feeling of excitement, as if they "knew" they were doing the right thing.
4. Theory. A primary goal often was to understand or explain something. Theoretical understanding seems to be a primary goal of significant research.
5. Real World. Often the research problem had an applied, real-world flavor to it or arose from contact with individuals with real problems.

Not-so-significant research, on the other hand, was characterized by the following attributes:

1. Expedience. The research project was easy, cheap, quick, or convenient. Genuine contributions apparently take substantial thought and effort.
2. Method. A method to be used took priority over theory and understanding. The purpose of the study was to try out a methodological technique. Even if published, the outcome was not very important.
3. Motivation. The investigators were not motivated by a desire for knowledge and understanding of some organizational phenomenon. The research was done primarily to get published or for money.
4. Lack of Theory. Not enough thought was provided in the study. Without theory, the research may be easier and quicker, but the outcome will often be insignificant.

Based on this study, Campbell et al. suggest some guidelines for significant research.

1. Significant research is an outcome of investigator involvement in the physical and social world of organizations.
2. Significant research is an outcome of investigator interest, resolve, and effort.
3. Significant research projects are chosen on the basis of intuition.
4. Significant research is an outcome of intellectual rigor.
5. Significant research reaches into the uncertain world of organizations and returns with something clear, tangible, and well understood.
6. Significant research focuses on real problems.
7. Significant research is concerned with theory, with a desire for understanding, and with explanation.

While this study was focused on organizational behavior and based on a small sample, it does suggest some important themes. Principally, research must be carried out in a careful and structured approach. It is to this end that the creative problem-solving process can provide important benefits.

Based on these results, several suggestions can be made for improving research effectiveness.

1. Develop a thorough understanding of a subject. You must demonstrate understanding of a subject, not just think that you possess it. Gaps in knowledge quickly surface when teaching a course. Writing a critical review of a body of literature is another useful means of increasing understanding.
2. Gain a wider variety of experience. This is an important theme in creativity and is supported by the Campbell et al. study. Attending professional conferences, eating lunch with colleagues and students, having periodic seminars, increasing interdisciplinary contacts, and working or consulting in organizations are useful strategies for doing this.
3. Use creativity stimulants.

Using Creativity Stimulants for Research Problem Identification

Many creativity stimulants can be used to identify ideas for research. Brainstorming is a common approach used in universities and research laboratories. The "Friday afternoon seminar" increases interaction among researchers, helps them to focus on the real issues in a research area, and suggests alternative methods of analysis.

Osborn's checklist provides a useful starting point for stimulating ideas. For example, consider any published research paper. One might ask the following questions. How can these results be **put to other uses**, perhaps in another discipline? Can I **adapt** these results to another problem? How can I **modify** the assumptions of the research? Can I **magnify** the model by adding new variables or constraints? Can I **minify** the model through aggregation? Can I **substitute** a change of variables and reformulate the model to simplify it? Can I **rearrange** steps in the algorithm? How might I **reverse** the conclusions to generate new hypotheses? Can I **combine** these results with other published results? Such a checklist can provide numerous ideas for incremental research topics.

The forced-relationship techniques can be useful in the merging, creative application, and emerging discipline strategies. For example, one may classify heuristic approaches to optimization problems in the following categories:[21]

1. construction
2. improvement
3. decomposition
4. partitioning
5. mathematical programming
6. analytical approximation

If one develops a parallel list of applications, such as the traveling salesman problem, integer programming, scheduling, and so on, then a forced relationship between the heuristic approaches and the applications provides numerous ideas for new algorithmic solutions.

Attribute listing provides another approach for identifying incremental research ideas. For example, take a recently published model and list all of its attributes. A queueing model, for instance, might involve a Poisson arrival rate, exponential service rate, and a single channel. One might ask what the sensitivity to departures from a Poisson arrival assumption is in the model results. Or, what if we change from a single to multiple channels?

Morphological analysis is similar to attribute listing, but along multiple dimensions. For example, an inventory application might involve the attributes of demand (deterministic or stochastic, independent or dependent, static or dynamic), number of items (one or many), lead time (deterministic or stochastic), and stockouts (backorders or lost sales). Every combination of these characteristics provides a new problem scenario and opportunity for model building or solution. (This technique also provides a convenient way to classify existing literature to determine gaps in existing knowledge.)

EXERCISES

1. Sample ten journal articles over the last five years in a single topic area. Write down the research questions that were addressed and investigated.

*2.   Describe the research currently being performed in your area of interest. What is interesting about this research to you?

3.   Interview faculty members or practitioners in your field. Attempt to determine the most important needs in a research area and contrast these needs to what actually has been studied by researchers.

4.   Ask faculty members to describe a study that they are most proud of and one that they are not so proud of and would rather forget. Determine the origins of the research questions that were studied. Can you find distinct themes that characterize important research from not-so-important research?

*5.   Examine a research paper from a recent journal and attempt to classify the research using Osborn's checklist. Do any new categories arise?

*6.   Using the *titles* of research papers alone, classify one issue of *Management Science* according to the various strategies presented in this chapter (that is, the incremental strategy, merging strategy, and so on).

ENDNOTES

1.   W.C. Emory, *Business Research Methods*, 3d ed. (Homewood, IL: Richard D. Irwin, 1985).

2.   See John D.C. Little, "Research Opportunities in the Decision and Management Sciences," *Management Science* 32, no. 1 (January 1986): pp. 1–13 for a discussion of research opportunities that fall within the DMS program.

3.   Historical facts were cited by Alex Osborn in *Applied Imagination* (New York: Charles Scribner's Sons, 1953 and revised editions).

4.   An excellent book describing the research process in depth is Uma Sekaran, *Research Methods for Managers: A Skill-Building Approach* (New York: John Wiley & Sons, 1984).

5.   Jack R. Meredith et al., "Alternative Research Paradigms in Operations," *Journal of Operations Management*, 8, no. 4 (October 1989): pp. 297–326. The authors provide an excellent discussion of research paradigms—that is, sets of methods that all exhibit the same pattern or elements in common, with examples drawn from operations management.

6.   R. Dubin, *Theory Building* (New York: The Free Press, 1969).

7.   John P. Campbell, Richard L. Daft, and Charles L. Hulin, *What To Study: Generating and Developing Research Questions* (Beverly Hills: Sage Publications, 1982).

8.   Thomas L. Saaty, "Some Thoughts on Creativity," Chapter 12 in *Mathematical Methods of Operations Research* (New York: McGraw-Hill, 1959).

9. B.O. Koopman, "New Mathematical Methods in Operations Research," *Journal of the Operations Research Society of America* 1, no. 1 (November 1952): pp. 3–9.

10. Lawrence S. Kubie, "Blocks to Creativity," in Ross L. Mooney and Taher A. Razik, *Explorations in Creativity* (New York: Harper & Row, 1967).

11. R. Coile, "Ages of Creativeness of Electronic Engineers," Letter to the Editor, *Proceedings of the Institute of Radio Engineers* 42, no. 8 (August, 1954): pp. 1322–23, and H.C. Lehman, *Age and Achievement* (Princeton, NJ: Princeton University Press, 1953).

12. William D. Hitt and John R. Stock, "The Relation Between Psychological Characteristics and Creative Behavior," in Mooney and Razik, *Explorations in Creativity*, pp. 259–66.

13. See Little, "Research Opportunities," for a discussion of research issues in DS/MS; Christian Scholz, "OR/MS Methodology—A Conceptual Framework," *OMEGA, The International Journal of Management Science* 12, no. 1: pp. 53–61, for an example in the operations research field; and C.A. Voss, "Production/Operations Management—A Key Discipline and Area for Research," *OMEGA, The International Journal of Management Science* 12, no. 3 (1984): pp. 309–319, and Elwood S. Buffa, "Research in Operations Management," *Journal of Operations Management* 1 (1980): pp. 1–8, for examples in the P/OM area.

14. Richard B. Chase "A Classification and Evaluation of Research in Operations Management," *Journal of Operations Management* 1, no. 1 (1980): pp. 9–14.

15. Harish C. Bahl, Larry P. Ritzman, and Jatinder N.D. Gupta, "Determining Lot Sizes and Resource Requirements: A Review," *Operations Research* 35, no. 3 (May-June 1987): pp. 329–45.

16. Wilse B. Webb, "The Choice of the Problem," *American Psychologist* 16 (1961): pp. 223–27.

17. Meredith et al., "Alternative Research Paradigms in Operations."

18. This section is adapted in part from Arnold Reisman, "On Alternative Strategies for Doing Research in the Management and Social Sciences," *IEEE Transactions on Engineering Management* 35, no. 4 (1988): pp. 215–220, and from S.C. Narula, "Guidelines for Identifying Research Problems in Operations Research," unpublished manuscript.

19. Robert D. Plante, "The Nozzle Guide Vane Problem," *Operations Research* 36, no. 1 (January-February 1988): pp. 18–33.

20. Campbell et al., *What to Study*.

21. S.H. Zanakis, J.R. Evans, and A.A. Vazacopoulos, "Heuristic Methods and Applications: A Categorized Survey," *European Journal of Operational Research* 43 (1989): pp. 88–110.

EPILOG
Educational Implications of Creative Thinking

Educating oneself, or others, to be more creative involves first, understanding what creativity is and, second, practicing creativity. Isaksen and Parnes propose some assumptions appropriate for creative learning:[1]

1. The student should go to school to acquire skills that enable him or her to continue learning to deal with unknown and unpredicted events and challenges. Part of these skills involves the ability to acquire knowledge necessary for the task at hand. In Chapter 1 we argued the need for creativity by addressing the fact that the world is changing rapidly and that we now face more ill-structured problems than ever before. We can no longer rely on knowledge that has existed for a long time and is simply handed down.

2. Specific subject matter provides the raw material for learning but has value only when put to use in relevant and meaningful ways. "Rote" learning will not help us to tackle the problems that we will face in the future.

3. The best way to attain knowledge is through active, experiential learning in a setting meaningful to the individual. No longer can knowledge be acquired through unassociated fragments. Case studies and "capstone" experiences are important means of doing this.

4. What is relevant, meaningful, and sensible to the learner varies according to each individual's background, experience, character-

161

istics, and needs. Teachers have different perspectives from students and need to recognize this. Moreover, we are discovering that the average student learns in ways different from the teacher, particularly if that teacher is in a technical area and the student is not.

5. Education involves growth and is therefore a component of living. The knowledge acquired by the average engineer is obsolete within five years. Education is not simply a preparation for life; it must be continually developed.

6. Personally meaningful learning involves interaction and effective communication with others. Active involvement through cases and real projects, for example, is critical to education.

7. The learner's needs and involvement provide the initial purpose for creative learning. The teacher cannot determine the purpose of learning.

8. It is important to involve the learner in choosing tasks that are interesting and have relevance, or to find ways of making given tasks interesting or purposeful to the learner.

9. While solutions to problems may have immediate importance, learning a problem-solving process has great long-range importance. As we stated earlier in this book, it is the process, not the end product, that often provides the greater benefit to the decision maker.

10. It is both possible and important to document the impact and value of creative learning, rather than simply measuring what has been learned.

Think back on your own education. How do these points relate to how you were taught? If you are a professor or graduate student, how do they relate to you *now*?

ENDNOTE

1.   Scott G. Isaksen and Sidney J. Parnes, "Curriculum Planning for Creative Thinking and Problem Solving, *Journal of Creative Behavior* 19, no. 1 (1985): pp. 1–29.

Index